The Newlywed Kitchen

THE NEWLYWED KITCHEN

Delicious Meals for Couples Cooking Together

Lorna Yee and Ali Basye

SASQUATCH
BOOKS

Printed in China
Published by Sasquatch Books
Distributed by PGW/Perseus
15 14 13 12 11   9 8 7 6 5 4 3 2

Cover design: Kate Basart/Union Pageworks
Cover photographs: Kathryn Barnard
Interior design and composition: Kate Basart/Union Pageworks
Interior photographs: Kathryn Barnard and Lorna Yee

Library of Congress Cataloging-in-Publication Data is available.

ISBN-13: 978-1-57061-632-7

SASQUATCH BOOKS | 119 South Main Street, Suite 400 | Seattle, WA 98104
206/467-4300 | www.sasquatchbooks.com | custserv@sasquatchbooks.com

Contents

Preface

"HAVE NO FEAR AND FOLLOW NO RULES. DON'T EVEN
THINK ABOUT WHAT'S PROPER OR WHAT'S RIGHT OR
WHAT'S WRONG. WHETHER YOUR FOOD IS GREAT OR NOT IS
UNIMPORTANT. WHAT *IS* IMPORTANT IS CREATING MEMORIES."
—*Kimberly Paley, co-owner, Paley's Place, Portland, Oregon*

Have no fear" could summarize the theme of this book, a project that grew from a desire to inspire newlyweds to learn to love cooking together and create a place of harmony in the kitchen.

"But couples don't get along in the kitchen!" you may insist. I often heard that line when sharing the idea about this book. As evidence, skeptics shared their horror stories of intimidating alpha-behavior, culinary performance anxiety, and cooking disasters that damaged confidence. But there were others, those who understood that cooking with one's spouse and sitting down to a meal together is one of the most enjoyable, intimate—and yes, sometimes daring—activities a couple can share, and who do so with their partner nearly every day. These couples have no fear in the kitchen and take great pleasure in decompressing at the end of the day as they create a shared expression of love and gratitude.

Finding the time is another big argument against cooking from scratch, but I am a firm believer that the benefits of slowing down to prepare a plate of food override the convenience—and cost—of mindlessly consuming packaged, processed, and fast foods. Cooking, whether putting together a simple snack or a multicourse meal, is a terrific way to shake off the stress of a day and connect with the person you love. And if that doesn't convince you, I gathered what I call "food-love stories" from some of the busiest couples there are: those working in the food industry. Throughout the pages of *The Newlywed Kitchen*, these couples—from food writers, executive chefs, and sommeliers to ranchers—share memories of discovering food with their spouses. Their stories run the gamut from funny to romantic, but all are linked by the common thread that sharing a meal and cooking with (or for) your spouse is an integral and exciting part of the relationship.

In the eleven years I've worked with newlyweds, more than a few times couples have (laughingly) told me that culinary-themed wedding presents are the first items they return for cash, that they only use the kitchen for storage, or that they've never once cooked a meal together. I believe that a dependence on eating preprepared foods stems more from a fear of failure, lack of inspiration, or the absence of existing culinary traditions than a simple aversion to the idea. And so Lorna Yee, a Seattle cook and food writer who is also a newlywed, created approachable, delicious recipes that couples of all

skill levels can tackle. In addition, each section contains a menu that will draw upon your culinary skills and serve as the foundation for creating meals for memorable occasions.

A new marriage is a fresh start, an opportunity to launch new traditions and share ones from your past. To wit, one of our story contributors, Kate McDermott, perhaps America's foremost apple pie guru, offered this gem when discussing her relatively new marriage with food luminary Jon Rowley: "He had a history with food; I have a history of cooking with my family; and now we have a shared history. Our relationship and marriage is punctuated and enriched by our adventures and explorations of food."

That last line could be the essence of this book. Through cooking, you too can discover your shared culinary histories, make them your own, and enrich your lives.

—*Ali Basye*

Introduction

I wrote the recipes for *The Newlywed Kitchen* during my first year of marriage to my husband, Henry, a wonderful man who shares my love of good food. Much of our relationship has revolved around the enjoyment of cooking together, and for one another, which should come as no surprise, considering we met on an Internet cooking forum.

Back in 2006, Henry was a new member on eGullet.org, an international food board where avid home cooks, bakers, restaurant professionals, and diners convened to review their favorite restaurants, discuss various cooking techniques, and ask for cooking advice. At the time, Henry was chosen to blog about his city, Seattle, for one week. Each day, Henry posted a breathtaking photographic journal that included tasting menus at his favorite restaurants, an array of photos from famed Pike Place Market, and a casual *Sopranos*-themed potluck with his friends. Thousands of us tuned in that week to watch this young man's enthusiastic take on the Seattle food scene, and I was one in the happy chorus of fans.

Near the end of his weeklong blogging stint, I mentioned that I was hoping to try a couple of the Seattle restaurants he had profiled (in particular, one that served gorgeous little desserts). I was already planning on flying out of Seattle to have dinner at The French Laundry with some friends. (That visit to French Laundry—one of the best, and priciest, restaurants in the country—was an experience I had saved up for for many years, as I was a poor college student at the time.) Reservations are notoriously difficult to come by, and Henry politely emailed to see if he could tag along. As luck would have it, we did have an extra seat at the table. I met Henry the following week, and he took me on a whirlwind eating tour in Seattle that spanned five restaurants over the course of one day, ending in a private dessert-tasting menu at what would soon become our special restaurant.

Before he drove me home to Vancouver, BC, Henry gave me a box of desserts he had asked his pastry chef friend to make—the very desserts he photographed for his blog. They say the way to a man's heart is through his stomach—well, I guess you could say the same is true for me. I was smitten, both by Henry's thoughtfulness and by his love for good food.

In the year and a half before we got engaged at that same special restaurant Henry took me to on our first date, we celebrated many of our milestones at the stove. For our first Thanksgiving, we hosted a potluck, challenged one another to a prepared turkey competition, and had our forty friends choose a winner. We've made burgers for a rooftop Fourth of July to feed a hundred; we've made special candlelit meals at home just for the two of us. On the night Henry asked me to be his wife, the first serious discussion we had (after a bit of tipsy celebrating) was about what we should serve at the wedding. For our honeymoon, we decided to go on a whirlwind eating tour of Chicago, and we

proceeded to eat at fourteen restaurants in three days. For our first Christmas as a married couple in our "new" (rundown, fixer-upper) home, we roasted little Cornish game hens, opened a good bottle of wine, and held hands at a makeshift table while sitting on folding chairs. Whatever the circumstance, we have always enjoyed cooking together and feeding one another. Dinnertime is a sacred time for us—a time to feed our bellies as well as our souls.

I look forward to a lifetime filled with delicious dinners alongside my dear husband, and I hope this cookbook will inspire that same love of preparing and sharing good food for all couples.

—Lorna Yee

Carry Me Over the Threshold

STARTERS & SNACKS

Prosciutto, Sage, and Parmesan Pinwheels

Henry's Famous Spicy Wings

Zucchini Fritters with Tangy Yogurt Sauce

Roasted Tomatillo Salsa

Bacon, Onion, and Pecorino Mini Quiches

Blue Cheese Crackers

Chicken and Chorizo Empanadas

"ALWAYS MAKE TIME TO EAT TOGETHER. IT'S FUN AND ENJOYABLE—IT'S SENSUAL, ACTUALLY."

—*Armandino Batali, founder of Salumi in Seattle, Washington*

PROSCIUTTO, SAGE, AND PARMESAN PINWHEELS

Makes about 28 pinwheels

Serve these easy-to-make pinwheels at your first gathering as newlyweds for a crisp, two-bite popper that pairs beautifully with bubbly. They look "gourmet" but are a breeze to put together: I prepared them with our friends' 2-year-old daughter, Maysun, who adores helping me in the kitchen. If she can do it, so can you!

> **1 sheet puff pastry, defrosted**
> **3 heaping tablespoons honey mustard**
> **3 ounces thinly sliced prosciutto**
> **1 tablespoon finely chopped fresh sage**
> **$3/4$ cup grated Parmesan**
> **$1/4$ teaspoon freshly ground black pepper**

1. On a lightly floured surface, unfold the puff pastry sheet and roll it into a rectangle measuring 11 by 14 inches. Spread the mustard evenly over the entire surface and arrange the prosciutto evenly on top of the mustard. Sprinkle the sage, Parmesan, and pepper evenly over the prosciutto. Roll up one side of the pastry toward the center, jelly roll style, stopping in the middle. Repeat this step on the other side so that the two rolls meet in the center.

2. Carefully wrap the pastry in plastic wrap to help retain its shape. Refrigerate for 3 hours (or overnight) so the pastry has a chance to firm up. (If you're in a rush, you can instead freeze the dough for about 30 minutes.)

3. Preheat the oven to 400°F.

4. With a serrated knife, slice the roll into $1/2$-inch pieces and place them on a parchment- or Silpat-lined baking sheet, leaving a bit of space between the pieces so they have room to puff up as they bake. Bake the pinwheels for 15 to 17 minutes, or until they are golden and crisp. Serve warm or at room temperature with glasses of bubbly.

PROSCIUTTO, SAGE,
AND PARMESAN
PINWHEELS

HENRY'S FAMOUS SPICY WINGS

Makes about 48 wings

My husband, Henry, is known for his hot wings—we even served these at our bridal shower! The reason they are so addictive is that they're twice baked, so the sauce caramelizes onto the wings. A final sprinkle of buttery breadcrumbs gives them some extra crunch without deep-frying. I joke that I married Henry so I'd have lifetime access to this recipe. And now we're passing it on to you!

> **4 pounds chicken wings**
> **6 tablespoons unsalted butter, divided**
> **1 cup hot sauce, such as Frank's Redhot**
> **3 tablespoons *sriracha****
> **3 tablespoons *sambal oelek****
> **¼ cup packed dark brown sugar**
> **¾ cup panko (or substitute regular bread crumbs)**

1. Preheat the oven to 425°F.

2. Arrange the wings in a single layer on two baking trays. (Make sure the trays have slightly raised edges, to catch the grease.) Bake the wings for 40 minutes, or until they are golden.

3. Meanwhile, in a large skillet over medium heat, melt 5 tablespoons of the butter. Stir in the hot sauce, *sriracha*, *sambal oelek*, and brown sugar and heat for 5 to 7 minutes, or until the sugar has melted and the sauce is warm.

4. In a separate skillet over medium-high heat, melt the remaining butter. Toast the panko, stirring frequently, until it is golden brown and crisp, about 3 minutes.

5. When the wings are cooked, pour the drippings into the hot sauce mixture and stir to combine. Toss the wings in the hot sauce, then arrange them again in a single layer on the baking trays. Reserve the remaining hot sauce.

6. Bake the wings for 12 minutes, or until the sauce is caramelized and the wings lightly crisped. Toss the coated wings again in the reserved hot sauce and sprinkle with panko before serving.

---

* *These Asian hot sauces should be available in the ethnic section of your grocery store or at any Asian supermarket.*

Starters & Snacks

A Moveable Feast

❧✦❧

MARILYN AND ARMANDINO BATALI, FOUNDERS
OF SALUMI IN SEATTLE, WASHINGTON

Married: December 26, 1959

D o you remember on our honeymoon when we ran out of food?"
Armandino Batali asks, turning to Marilyn, his wife of fifty years.
They are sitting in a small room at the back of their esteemed
deli, Salumi, noshing on sweet and salty antipasti and drinking wine from
cups. Parents of three children, including famed chef Mario Batali, the
couple recounts early memories of their marriage and how they happily
made do with very little.

"We got married the day after Christmas and drove down the coast to
see Washington in the Rose Bowl," Armandino explains. "We had this
little Renault, and we made it to Redding before we ran out of cash."

"I remember. We were in Santa Rosa," Marilyn continues. "The artichoke capital. It was New Year's Eve so I went into a shop and bought a
piece of turkey. We boiled turkey on the little cooktop in the motel room
and picked olives along the roadside—you couldn't even eat them, really—
and that was our feast!"

"We set out for a romantic honeymoon and ended up with stolen
olives!" Armandino says, breaking into laughter.

"One of the things that is different now is that back then we ate seasonally," Marilyn recalls. "You'd go along the ditch and find asparagus,
greens, herbs—in fact, we just stole some mint not too long ago!"

"It's not *stealing*," Armandino chuckles.

"There used to be a time when you could feast on oysters from Puget
Sound and go clam digging and take home all you wanted. You didn't
need a lot of money to eat well," Marilyn continues.

"Back then if we wanted fresh items, we'd pick 'em, or grow 'em, or steal 'em!" Armandino declares proudly.

"But we always took time to cook and sit down at the table," Marilyn says. "We might not have been sophisticated in the early days, but cooking—simple and clean flavors—has always been a priority."

"We always enjoyed each other in the kitchen," Armandino concurs. "For us, that was dating. There was a true compatibility about food then, and there still is today."

ADVICE FOR NEWLYWEDS: *Just love cooking: the simpler, the better. It doesn't have to be fancy, especially when you're first married.*

—Armandino

FAVORITE THINGS IN THE KITCHEN: *A good sauté pan and a Cuisinart.*

—Armandino and Marilyn

ZUCCHINI FRITTERS WITH TANGY YOGURT SAUCE

Makes 10 fritters

Looking for an easy way to incorporate more vegetables into your day? These zucchini fritters come together in less than fifteen minutes and pair wonderfully with Sweet-and-Hot Chicken Kebabs (page 126). These versatile fritters are especially tasty when topped with Tangy Yogurt Sauce, but also try them with Romesco Sauce (page 108).

3 cups (about 2 large) grated zucchini
$1/2$ teaspoon kosher salt
2 cloves garlic, finely minced
1 large egg
$1/4$ teaspoon freshly ground black pepper
$1/4$ cup grated Parmesan
$1/2$ cup flour
3 tablespoons extra-virgin olive oil
Tangy Yogurt Sauce (recipe follows)

1. Combine the zucchini and salt in a sieve positioned over a large bowl and squeeze the water out with your hands. (You should be able to remove about $1/2$ cup of water.)

2. Transfer the zucchini to a large bowl and add the garlic, egg, pepper, Parmesan, and flour. Stir to combine.

3. Heat the olive oil in a large skillet over medium-high heat. Spoon heaping tablespoons of the zucchini batter into the pan, making sure the fritters don't touch one another. Brown the fritters for about 3 minutes, lifting the edge to check on the color. When the fritters are golden brown, flip and cook for another 2 to 3 minutes. Serve the fritters warm, topped with the Tangy Yogurt Sauce.

ZUCCHINI FRITTERS
WITH TANGY
YOGURT SAUCE

TANGY YOGURT SAUCE

Makes ¾ cup of sauce

¾ cup plain Greek yogurt

1 teaspoon freshly squeezed lemon juice

1 tablespoon chopped fresh parsley

Kosher salt and freshly ground black pepper

1. In a small bowl, stir together the yogurt, lemon juice, parsley, and salt and pepper to taste.

ROASTED TOMATILLO SALSA

Makes 2½ cups of salsa

Fresh, homemade tomatillo salsa, with a side of sour cream and a bowl of tortilla chips, is always welcome, whether you are entertaining friends or just having a quiet movie night with your sweetie. Best of all, this recipe comes together in about fifteen minutes—instant gratification!

> 1 pound fresh tomatillos
> 4 serrano chilies, stemmed
> 1 tablespoon extra-virgin olive oil
> 1 medium sweet yellow onion, finely diced
> 3 cloves garlic, finely chopped
> ⅓ cup fresh cilantro, chopped
> ¼ cup water
> 2 tablespoons freshly squeezed lime juice
> Zest of 1 medium lime (about ½ teaspoon)
> 1 teaspoon sugar (optional)
> Kosher salt and freshly ground black pepper

1. Preheat the broiler.

2. Arrange the tomatillos and chilies on a parchment- or Silpat-lined baking sheet. Broil for 4 to 5 minutes per side, until the tops are charred and the skins begin to split.

3. Meanwhile, heat the olive oil in a large skillet over medium-high heat. Add the onions and sauté for 5 to 6 minutes, until they are softened and lightly caramelized. Add the garlic and cook for another minute.

4. In a food processor or blender, combine the tomatillos, chilies, onions, garlic, cilantro, water, lime juice, and lime zest. Pulse until smooth. Add the sugar. Season with salt and pepper to taste, and pulse again to combine.

5. Serve the salsa right away or keep it covered and refrigerated for up to 4 days.

Starters & Snacks

11

Romaine Holiday

❧✦❧

KATHY CASEY, CHEF AND AUTHOR OF NINE
COOKBOOKS, AND HER HUSBAND, JOHN,
PARTNERS IN KATHY CASEY FOOD STUDIOS-
LIQUID KITCHEN AND DISH D'LISH

Married: August 15, 1981

For a couple who've made a career out of the art of celebrating, it's no surprise that John and Kathy Casey's nonprofessional lives are also brimming with joyful, romantic stories—almost all of which involve food.

"On one of our early dates, I wooed him with food," laughs Kathy, one of the country's first female executive chefs. "I just came up with the menu as I shopped around town—on the bus, I might add—and found seasonal ingredients I liked. It took me all day, but I really wanted to impress him!"

"It worked," John laughs, and the pair launch into the details of the multicourse French meal the 17-year-old budding chef cooked in her tiny apartment kitchen more than three decades prior: Coquilles St. Jacques, various decadent dishes featuring rich sauces, and elaborate desserts.

That style of no-fear cooking was great practice for Kathy's career and also for the kind of gourmet meals on the fly the couple have relished since then. Finishing each other's sentences, they relay story after story, such as a particularly memorable picnic of foraged wild mushrooms, ripe huckleberries, and crisp field greens.

Another time they celebrated the Christmas holiday in a small inn alongside Florence's picturesque Ponte Vecchio. Knowing that the restaurants would close and they'd need to fend for themselves, the couple got permission to use the inn's tiny kitchen and spent Christmas Eve day scouring the markets, buying simple ingredients to put their own twist on the Italian holiday feast.

"It puts a smile on my face every time I remember it," John says. "There were no tourists left in the city, just Kathy and I wandering through the decorated town center and buying all this wonderful, simple peasant food. That night we shelled beans in our room and watched Italian TV, laughing and laughing. It was the most lovely experience."

The couple ate a delicious meal of steamed greens and vegetables, fresh dates, tossed salad, dried meats, cheeses, olives, crusty bread, and a few bottles of wine. Across the square the church bells of Santa Maria Novella chimed, and the couple felt like characters in an old movie.

"It was magical," Kathy remembers, "but also very low-key and no pressure. We just did our own thing and created something together. That always makes for the best memories."

ADVICE FOR NEWLYWEDS: *"Whatever you do as a couple, whether it's cooking or facing any kind of challenge together, you just have to go for it. You'll only succeed if you take risks and trust each other to be who you are."*

—*Kathy*

FAVORITE THING IN THE KITCHEN: *"Cocktails!"*

—*Kathy*

BACON, ONION, AND PECORINO MINI QUICHES

Makes 8 mini quiches

Everyone adores a good quiche, but the pastry can be intimidating for those just starting out in the kitchen. Using standard-size muffin tins and ready-made puff pastry makes these a snap to put together, and the savory flavors of bacon, onion, and cheese make them a classic. These five-bite quiches are the perfect little pastry for brunch, a late-afternoon snack, or a cocktail party.

> 1 tablespoon extra-virgin olive oil
>
> 5 strips bacon, cut into $\frac{1}{4}$-inch dice
>
> $\frac{3}{4}$ cup (about 1 medium) finely diced sweet yellow onion
>
> $\frac{1}{2}$ cup heavy cream
>
> $\frac{1}{8}$ teaspoon kosher salt
>
> $\frac{1}{8}$ teaspoon freshly ground black pepper
>
> $\frac{1}{2}$ teaspoon finely chopped fresh thyme
>
> $\frac{3}{4}$ cup grated pecorino (or substitute Parmesan or Gruyère)
>
> 1 large egg
>
> 1 egg yolk
>
> 1 sheet puff pastry (preferably made with butter), defrosted

1. Preheat the oven to 350°F.

2. Heat the olive oil in a large skillet over medium-high heat. Add the bacon and cook until it just begins to crisp, 3 to 4 minutes. Add the onions and cook until they begin to caramelize, 5 to 6 minutes.

3. Using a slotted spoon, transfer the bacon and onion mixture to a large bowl. Pour in the heavy cream and add the salt, pepper, and thyme. Stir in the pecorino and then add the egg and egg yolk. Give the mixture a final stir to make sure everything is incorporated.

4. On a lightly floured surface, unfold the puff pastry sheet. Using a floured rolling pin, roll the pastry to a thickness of $\frac{1}{8}$ inch. Using a floured 4-inch-round pastry cutter (or a glass about the same diameter, turned upside down), cut 8 circles. Fit each pastry round into a muffin cup, using your fingers to push the pastry into the bottom and up the sides of each cup. Fill the cups $\frac{3}{4}$ of the way with the egg custard.

5. Bake the quiches for 30 to 35 minutes, or until the pastry is golden brown and the custard puffs slightly. Let the quiches cool in the muffin tin for 5 minutes before releasing (they should pop right out).

An Unlikely Pairing

❧ 🌿 ❧

SALLY MOHR, MASTER SOMMELIER, AND
HER HUSBAND, CARL, PROPRIETORS OF
THE BOULDER WINE MERCHANT

Married: June 8, 1980

The adage about happy accidents has rarely been truer than following the wedding of master sommelier Sally Mohr and her husband, Carl. The couple had booked a room in an airport hotel—the better to catch their early-morning honeymoon flight—and arrived there after the reception exhausted and hungry (because everyone knows you never eat at your own reception). Someone had gifted them with a bottle of champagne, and as they scanned the room service menu, nothing but a beef burrito seemed even remotely appetizing.

"I was still a few years away from my career in wine," says Sally, who became the second woman in the United States to achieve the level of master sommelier, "so maybe that's why I was willing to risk pairing champagne with a beef burrito. But darn, if those two didn't go really well together!"

Sally describes the clash of flavors that had her and Carl over the moon: the heavy cheese and beans against the dark meat and the champagne's bright acidity. "It's hard to believe," she says, "but you're cleansing the palate of heat and spice and lots of flavor—and it's really refreshing!"

So nearly every year since, Sally and Carl have marked the occasion with an anniversary meal of beef burritos and champagne—except that today the menu has become slightly more sophisticated.

"We use a good cut of meat, like rib eye," she says, "and a champagne with a high percentage of pinot noir, something with a rich body, age, and flavor to it, like a Charles Heidsieck rosé."

Ultimately, Sally says, enjoying wine and finding flavors that you like is all about experimentation. "Try something different once in a while," she says. "Don't be afraid to explore. You never know what you'll discover."

ADVICE FOR NEWLYWEDS: *"If you're eating regional or specialty food, think about the wine that is made in the same place as the food you are having. There is synergy in a place, and the flavors might work well together—despite my champagne-burrito combination!"*

—Sally

FAVORITE THINGS IN THE KITCHEN: *"A two-stage waiter's corkscrew with a double boot and a Microplane cheese grater."*

—Sally

BLUE CHEESE CRACKERS

Makes about 20 crackers

These blue cheese crackers, flavored with dry mustard and a bit of spicy cayenne, are the perfect addition to any cheese board. Try topping them with your favorite chutney and a soft cheese, such as Gorgonzola or Brie. Paired with wine, they are wonderful to have on hand when the in-laws drop by.

> 1 cup Stilton, crumbled, at room temperature
> 4 tablespoons (½ stick) unsalted butter, softened
> 1¾ cups flour
> ¼ teaspoon cayenne
> ¾ teaspoon dry mustard
> 1 tablespoon sugar
> ¾ teaspoon kosher salt
> 2 tablespoons heavy cream
> ¼ cup coarsely chopped walnuts or pecans

1. In a food processor, combine the Stilton and butter and pulse until well blended. Add the flour, cayenne, dry mustard, sugar, and salt and pulse until blended. Add the cream and pulse until the dough is smooth. Place the dough in a medium bowl and knead in the walnuts until incorporated.

2. On a lightly floured surface, roll the dough into a log about 2 inches in diameter and wrap tightly in plastic wrap. Gently squeeze the plastic wrap to smooth the log. Freeze the dough for 40 minutes.

3. Preheat the oven to 375°F.

4. Remove the plastic wrap, then slice the dough into ¼-inch rounds. Place the rounds on a parchment- or Silpat-lined baking sheet and bake for 22 to 25 minutes, or until they are golden brown. Transfer the crackers to a wire rack to cool. (The crackers will firm up once they've cooled.)

CHICKEN AND CHORIZO EMPANADAS

Makes 12 empanadas

Empanadas, those beloved handheld South American pastries, are often served as party appetizers—who doesn't love having a fried, portable snack in one hand and a beer in the other? The pastries are filled with a traditional mix of diced chicken, chorizo, olives, raisins, and spices. The savory/salty/sweet tastes play off one another, and a tiny splash of red wine vinegar at the end brightens the flavors. Invite friends over to enjoy them or plan a fiesta for two.

FOR THE CRUST:

2 cups flour

2 teaspoons baking powder

$^3/_4$ teaspoon kosher salt

$^1/_2$ cup lard, or 1 stick unsalted butter, cut into $^1/_4$-inch cubes

$^1/_2$ cup light beer

FOR THE FILLING:

2 tablespoons extra-virgin olive oil

1 medium onion, finely diced

2 cloves garlic, minced

$^1/_2$ cup ($2^1/_2$ ounces) diced chorizo

2 cups ($^1/_2$ pound) diced cooked chicken

$1^1/_2$ teaspoons sweet paprika

$^3/_4$ teaspoon ground cumin

$^1/_2$ cup kalamata olives, pitted and chopped

$^1/_2$ cup golden raisins, coarsely chopped

1 large hard-boiled egg, diced (optional, but traditional)

2 tablespoons dry sherry

$^2/_3$ cup chicken stock

2 tablespoons tomato paste

2 teaspoons red wine vinegar

Kosher salt and freshly ground black pepper

Starters & Snacks

1. To make the crust, in a large bowl, combine the flour, baking powder, and salt. Cut in the lard with a pastry blender or two knives, then stir in the beer. Knead the dough just until it comes together and then wrap in plastic wrap. Refrigerate the dough while you prepare the filling.

2. To make the filling, heat the olive oil in a large skillet over medium heat. Add the onions and sauté until golden brown, 7 to 8 minutes. Add the garlic, chorizo, chicken, paprika, cumin, olives, raisins, and egg. Cook for 4 or 5 minutes, until the filling is warmed through, then add the sherry, chicken stock, tomato paste, and red wine vinegar. Stir the mixture together until most of the liquid is absorbed, about 2 to 3 minutes. Season with salt and pepper to taste. Let the filling cool.

3. On a lightly floured surface, using a floured rolling pin, roll the dough to a thickness of $\frac{1}{8}$ inch. Using a floured 3-inch-round pastry cutter (or a glass of about the same diameter, turned upside down), cut 12 rounds of dough. Top the rounds with 1 heaping tablespoon of the filling, then fold to create half circles. Crimp the edges with a fork to seal. (If you have any leftover filling, simply toss it in a skillet with a couple of eggs for a yummy morning scramble.)

4. *To bake:* Place the empanadas on a parchment- or Silpat-lined baking sheet and bake in a preheated 375°F oven for 20 to 25 minutes, or until they are golden brown.
   To fry: Fill a heavy-bottomed, deep skillet with 1 inch of vegetable oil. Heat the oil over high heat until it registers 365°F on a deep-fat thermometer, then fry the empanadas in small batches, about 3 minutes per side, or until they are golden brown. Transfer to paper towels to drain briefly, then keep warm in the oven. Return oil to 365°F between batches.

MENU

A Housewarming Party

Prosciutto, Sage, and Parmesan Pinwheels, page 3

Bacon, Onion, and Pecorino Mini Quiches, page 14

Zucchini Fritters with Tangy Yogurt Sauce, page 8

Candy Bar Cupcakes, page 203

For Better or for Worse

BUDGET-FRIENDLY SOUPS, SALADS & SANDWICHES

Warm Mushroom Salad with Ginger Soy Vinaigrette

Curried Chickpea and Goat Cheese Salad

Supergooey Philly Cheesesteak Sliders

Anniversary Pea Soup with Seared Sea Scallops

Kale, White Bean, and Sausage Soup

The Ultimate Grilled Cheese

Roasted Tomato Soup with Rosemary Croutons

Pulled Pork Sandwiches

Bistro-Style French Onion Soup

Cuban Roast Sandwiches

"DON'T THINK OF FOODS THAT ARE OFF-LIMITS AS DENYING YOURSELF SOMETHING. INSTEAD SAY YES TO THE FOODS YOU *CAN* EAT, AND LEARN AS MUCH AS YOU CAN ABOUT THEM."

—*Shauna James Ahern, author of* Gluten-Free Girl

WARM MUSHROOM SALAD WITH GINGER SOY VINAIGRETTE

Serves 2

On those days when you're both tapped for time, this warm mushroom salad, topped with crisp bacon pieces and tossed in an Asian-inspired vinaigrette, is easy to throw together. Serve it with a bowl of soup and a nice piece of crusty, buttered baguette for a light and flavorful meal.

> 3 tablespoons extra-virgin olive oil, divided
> 4 strips bacon, cut into ¼-inch pieces
> 10 ounces (4 cups) mixed mushrooms, sliced
> 1 tablespoon soy sauce (or a dash more to taste)
> 2 teaspoons honey
> 2½ tablespoons rice wine vinegar
> 1 tablespoon finely grated peeled fresh ginger
> 2 tablespoons minced green onion
> 2 cups (about 1 bunch) packed baby spinach or arugula

1. Heat 1 tablespoon of the olive oil in a large skillet over medium-high heat. Add the bacon and cook until crisp, 3 to 4 minutes. Remove with a slotted spoon and place on paper towels to drain. Add the mushrooms to the bacon fat and sauté for 4 to 5 minutes, until the mushrooms are soft.

2. In a medium bowl, whisk together the remaining olive oil, soy sauce, honey, rice wine vinegar, ginger, and green onion. Pour the sauce over the mushrooms in the skillet, stir to coat, and allow the sauce to reduce for 30 seconds. In a separate bowl, toss the mushrooms and dressing with the spinach and bacon. Taste and adjust seasoning.

CURRIED CHICKPEA AND GOAT CHEESE SALAD

Serves 2

I love the taste of chickpeas, and the fact that they are high in protein and fiber makes them a healthful side dish any day of the week. This curried chickpea salad is bound by a creamy goat cheese dressing, thinned out with a bit of olive oil and fresh lemon juice. The best thing about it is that you can use it as a base for whatever leftovers you want to use up. Have some tomatoes and cucumbers instead of the red bell pepper? Feta instead of goat cheese? Those ingredients would also work nicely in this versatile salad.

> One 15-ounce can chickpeas, rinsed and drained
> 2 tablespoons finely minced shallots
> 2 roasted red bell peppers, cut into $1/4$-inch dice (about $1^{1}/_{2}$ cups)
> 2 tablespoons capers
> $1/4$ teaspoon kosher salt
> $1/8$ teaspoon freshly ground black pepper
> 3 tablespoons extra-virgin olive oil
> 3 tablespoons freshly squeezed lemon juice
> $1^{1}/_{4}$ teaspoons curry powder
> 2 tablespoons chopped fresh parsley
> 4 ounces goat cheese, crumbled

1. Combine all the ingredients in a medium bowl. Stir the mixture until the goat cheese breaks down and becomes a creamy sauce for the chickpeas.

2. Cover the salad in plastic wrap and refrigerate for at least 4 hours (preferably overnight) to let the flavors meld. Taste, and adjust for seasoning if necessary.

Soup à la Stowell

EXECUTIVE CHEF ETHAN STOWELL AND HIS
WIFE, ANGELA, CO-OWNERS OF FOUR SEATTLE
RESTAURANTS, INCLUDING TAVOLÀTA

Married: August 11, 2007

Many times, even the most stressful situations eventually become priceless family lore. In some cases those times even inspire new family traditions.

"Pretty much from the beginning, Ethan said he wanted to do all of the cooking," says Angela Stowell, reminiscing about her wedding day to her husband. "I asked him, 'Do you *really* want to cook for the wedding?'"

"And I said, 'Of course I do!'" Ethan laughs.

"We just wanted a very small wedding," Angela says, "very small with picnic kind of food."

"Just a small, food-centered wedding at sunset at my parents' place on Whidbey Island," Ethan adds.

"I was happy letting him plan the menu," Angela says, "but I did have one single request. What I really wanted was chilled corn soup in little demitasse cups."

"The day before the wedding I started prepping everything," Ethan says. "I made rib eyes, tomato salad, garden greens, vegetarian baked pasta—just tons of outdoor barbecue kind of food."

"I shucked the corn," Angela reminds him.

"Right. But then you were back at the inn getting ready for the rehearsal dinner. And my family started nagging me: 'It's time to go, we gotta go, you'll be late for your own rehearsal dinner!'"

"And you had enough time to make the soup, right?"

"Yeah, all I had left to do was blend the soup and leave," Ethan says, laughing now. "But it was typical Stowell family chaos. I'm looking for the blender and someone says, 'But there's no blender here!' And I just snapped. I grabbed the big pot of soup, and I walked out the back door to the edge of the cliff and just chucked it all over the side."

"All of my soup, over the cliff!" Angela says, laughing.

"I went back to the inn, and I had to tell her there wouldn't be any soup. The one thing she asked for she didn't get," Ethan says with a rueful smile.

"The next day I'm walking along the side of this cliff to get married in my wedding dress, and I'm walking past all this old corn soup," Angela says.

"That's how I deal with stuff; I throw stuff over the side of the cliff, and I move on," Ethan says.

"Exactly," Angela says. "So now we have a new family tradition. Every year on our anniversary we go to up to Whidbey Island, and we throw some corn over the cliff."

ADVICE FOR NEWLYWEDS: *"If it's not the best thing you've ever eaten, it's not a big deal. Make the whole cooking experience an event, including planning a menu and shopping together, so the process isn't only centered around the result."*

—Ethan

FAVORITE THINGS IN THE KITCHEN: *"A blender and a teapot."*

—Angela

"A really big pot and a good knife."

—Ethan

SUPERGOOEY PHILLY CHEESESTEAK SLIDERS

Makes 4 sliders

It's indisputable that a Philly cheesesteak is one of the greatest sandwiches in the world, and now neither of you have to fly to Philly and brave the crowds at Pat's or Geno's to get one. To cut really thin pieces of steak without a commercial meat slicer, just place the steak in the freezer for 45 to 60 minutes so it hardens slightly before you slice it. These sliders are packed full of a quarter pound of meat each! They're best eaten when you're both leaning over, elbows out, to preserve your center of gravity.

3 tablespoons vegetable oil, divided
1 medium sweet yellow onion, thinly sliced
2 cloves garlic, minced
1 thinly sliced bell pepper, any color
1 pound top round or rib eye, sliced as thinly as possible
2 teaspoons Worcestershire sauce
Kosher salt and freshly ground black pepper
6 ounces sharp provolone, or $^1/_3$ cup melted Cheez Whiz
4 mini hamburger buns

1. Heat 2 tablespoons of the vegetable oil in a large skillet over medium-high heat. Add the onions and sauté for 7 to 8 minutes, or until golden brown. Add the garlic and bell peppers, and cook for 2 to 3 minutes, or until the peppers are soft. Transfer the vegetables to a plate and set aside.

2. Add the remaining oil to the skillet. Cook the top round for 2 to 3 minutes, or until it is browned to your liking, then season it with the Worcestershire and salt and pepper to taste. Top the steak with the cheese and then the top buns (cut side down, facing the cheese), and cover the skillet with a lid for 1 to 2 minutes, or until the cheese has melted and the buns have warmed.

3. Pile the onions and peppers onto the bottom buns, then scoop the meat and cheese with bun on top.

ANNIVERSARY PEA SOUP WITH SEARED SEA SCALLOPS

Serves 2

My husband asked me to marry him at the same restaurant where we had our first date, a darling little French restaurant famed for its silky, sweet pea soup. The chef there served the soup in a very shallow dish, so you could see the large seared sea scallop floating in the center; the soup became a kind of luxurious, buttery pea sauce for the tender scallop. The restaurant became our special place where we celebrated all our milestones—sadly, it has closed its doors. Here is a simple pea soup we have at home whenever we want to recapture a bit of that romance.

FOR THE SOUP:

5 tablespoons unsalted butter, divided

2 medium shallots, finely diced

2¹/₂ cups fresh or frozen peas

2 cups vegetable stock

¹/₄ teaspoon dried piment d'Espelette* (or substitute a pinch of hot paprika)

Kosher salt

FOR THE SCALLOPS:

2 of the largest sea scallops you can find

Kosher salt

Dried piment d'Espelette or freshly ground black pepper

1 tablespoon unsalted butter

1 tablespoon extra-virgin olive oil

1. To make the soup, in a medium saucepan over medium heat, melt 3 tablespoons of butter. Add the shallots and sauté for 3 to 4 minutes, or until lightly brown. Add the peas and the vegetable stock. Simmer the peas for about 10 minutes, or until soft. Stir in the remaining butter and add the piment d'Espelette. Season with salt to taste.

---

* *Piment d'Espelette is a mild pepper from the Basque region of France, available online and possibly at your local gourmet grocery store.*

2.   Purée the soup with an immersion blender or in a food processor until smooth. Return the puréed soup to the pan, cover, and keep hot while you sear the scallops.

3.   To make the scallops, first remove the adductor muscles, if necessary. (The adductor is the roundish, slightly darker, tougher piece of meat attached to the scallop.) Pat the scallops dry and season them lightly with kosher salt and piment d'Espelette.

4.   In a small skillet over high heat, melt the butter and olive oil. Sear the scallops for about 2 minutes on the first side, and another 1 to 2 minutes on the other side. (You want a nice, evenly browned crust to form on both sides of the scallop.)

5.   Ladle the hot soup into two shallow dishes. Carefully place one scallop in the center of each dish, and garnish with a tiny bit of piment d'Espelette, if desired.

KALE, WHITE BEAN, AND SAUSAGE SOUP

Serves 2

The day my husband and I moved into our house, we took a break at lunch to explore our new neighborhood. We stumbled onto an ale house just two blocks away and had a restorative meal that included towering cider-braised pastrami sandwiches and the most fantastic kale, white bean, and sausage soup I'd ever tasted. When the ale house took the soup off the menu, I knew I had to make my own version at home. Cook this together for a meal that's both simple and satisfying.

1 tablespoon extra-virgin olive oil
¾ cup (about 1 medium) diced onion
½ pound mild Italian sausage, casings removed
1 bunch kale, chopped into ¾-inch pieces (about 3 cups)
One 14.5-ounce can diced tomatoes
Half a 15-ounce can cannellini beans
1 quart low-sodium chicken stock
½ teaspoon chopped fresh oregano
½ teaspoon ground cumin
1 bay leaf
1 Parmigiano-Reggiano rind, or 2 tablespoons grated Parmesan
Pinch of red pepper flakes (optional)
Kosher salt and freshly ground black pepper

1. Heat the olive oil in a large skillet over medium-high heat. Add the onions and sauté until golden brown, about 7 to 8 minutes. Brown the sausage with the onions, breaking up the meat with the spatula, 3 to 5 minutes.

2. In a stockpot, combine the sausage mixture with the rest of the ingredients. Bring to a boil over high heat, then lower the heat to medium-low and simmer, uncovered, for 30 to 60 minutes. (The longer you simmer the soup, the more flavorful it will become.) Remove the bay leaf and the Parmigiano rind before serving.

THE ULTIMATE GRILLED CHEESE

Makes 2 sandwiches

What sets this grilled cheese apart from any other you've ever had is its Parmesan crust—you butter the outside of the bread, sprinkle it with cheese, then grill the cheese directly onto the bread. Cheese inside and out? Now that's for the real hedonists!

> 4 tablespoons ($\frac{1}{2}$ stick) unsalted butter, softened, divided
> 4 slices sourdough bread
> $\frac{1}{4}$ cup grated Parmesan, divided
> $\frac{1}{4}$ teaspoon garlic salt
> $\frac{1}{4}$ teaspoon freshly ground black pepper
> 3 ounces Gorgonzola, cut into small pieces
> 4 ounces (about 1 cup) Gruyère, grated
> 4 slices tomato
> 1 tablespoon extra-virgin olive oil

1. Spread 1 tablespoon of butter on each slice of bread. Sprinkle 1 tablespoon of Parmesan on each slice, then distribute the garlic salt and pepper evenly over all the slices.

2. Flip two of the slices of bread over, and divide the Gorgonzola and Gruyère equally between them. Top each with 2 slices of tomato. Cover each sandwich half with the other slice of bread, with the Parmesan crust facing outward.

3. Lightly grease a small, heavy-bottomed skillet with the olive oil. Grill the sandwiches over medium heat until golden brown on both sides, about 3 minutes per side. Slice on the diagonal and serve.

ROASTED TOMATO SOUP WITH ROSEMARY CROUTONS

Serves 2

Tomato soup—creamy, tangy-sweet, and bursting with deep-roasted flavor—is high on everyone's comfort food list. Top each bowl with a small handful of these crunchy, garlic- and rosemary-scented croutons. This recipe may make a few more croutons than necessary for two portions, but they're so good, you'll find your-selves finishing them off after dinner.

1 pound large tomatoes
$1/4$ cup extra-virgin olive oil, divided
1 medium sweet yellow onion, diced
$1^1/2$ teaspoons dried marjoram
2 cloves garlic, finely minced
$1/3$ cup dry white wine
3 tablespoons tomato paste
$1^1/2$ cups low-sodium chicken stock
$1/2$ cup packed fresh basil
2 tablespoons heavy cream
Kosher salt and freshly ground black pepper
Rosemary Croutons (recipe follows)

1. Preheat the oven to 400°F.

2. Cut each tomato into six pieces and place them on a parchment- or Silpat-lined bak-ing sheet. Sprinkle 2 tablespoons of the olive oil over the tomatoes, and roast them for 25 minutes, or until the skins just start to pucker and curl.

3. Meanwhile, heat the remaining oil in a medium skillet over medium heat. Add the onions and sauté for 10 minutes, or until they turn golden brown. Add the marjoram and garlic. Add the white wine, stirring to pick up any of the brown bits on the bottom of the pan, and cook for 1 minute, or until most of the wine has evaporated.

4. Transfer the onion mixture to a stockpot and add the roasted tomatoes, tomato paste, chicken stock, basil, and heavy cream. Simmer the soup for 15 minutes, uncovered, then purée it with an immersion blender or in a food processor until smooth. Season with salt and pepper to taste. Ladle into bowls and top with Rosemary Croutons.

Budget-Friendly Soups, Salads & Sandwiches

ROSEMARY CROUTONS

ROSEMARY CROUTONS

Makes about 2 cups croutons

$^1/_3$ **cup extra-virgin olive oil**

1 sprig fresh rosemary

3 cloves garlic, chopped

2$^1/_2$ cups torn bread pieces (a baguette is best)

$^1/_2$ **teaspoon kosher salt**

$^1/_4$ **teaspoon freshly ground black pepper**

1. Preheat the oven to 350°F.

2. Heat the olive oil and rosemary together in a medium skillet over medium heat for 5 minutes to allow the rosemary to infuse the oil. Add the garlic and sauté for 1 minute. Add the bread pieces, salt, and pepper. Toss the bread pieces in the oil to coat, then transfer to a baking sheet. Toast the bread for 10 to 15 minutes, or until it is crisp and golden brown.

Wheat Not, Want Not

❧❦❧

SHAUNA JAMES AHERN, AUTHOR OF *GLUTEN-FREE GIRL*, AND HER HUSBAND, DANIEL

Married: July 16, 2007

After Shauna James Ahern was diagnosed with celiac disease—a digestive disorder that prevents the body from tolerating gluten—she waited almost a year before dating again. Her reasoning was that she had been sick for so long before her diagnosis that she wanted to spend time with her now healthy self before she brought someone new into her life. So she spent a year learning to live without wheat and teaching herself to prepare and cook gluten-free food.

And then she met Dan, a professional chef.

"Food was our profound connection," Shauna says. "Danny never saw gluten free as a roadblock, but as a challenge. He loves to cook for me and watch me enjoy his food!"

In fact, Dan started preparing gluten-free meals at the Seattle restaurant where he worked because, he says, "I wanted Shauna to be able to eat everything I made."

Food made with love, Shauna notes, can inspire very intense feelings. One afternoon the couple came home from grocery shopping ("pure foreplay for us," Shauna laughs), and Dan prepared a simple dish he knew she would love: a French frisée salad with warm bacon vinaigrette.

"With that one first bite, I didn't know food could be so good. I turned to him and blurted out, 'Oh, just move in with me!' " Shauna remembers. "In this case, the taste of the food spoke for us both. The flavors created a sensuality and a connection that was undeniable."

Shauna had already begun documenting her life as a gluten-free girl on her blog, and soon Dan and their love affair with each other and food made their way into the posts. Now married, the couple has a baby daughter and a best-selling book, both of which are covered on the blog, and a gluten-free cookbook is on the way.

"Cooking is a great way to feed each other with love, not just with food," Dan says. "Food is the essence of how we enjoy life together."

ADVICE FOR NEWLYWEDS: *"Don't relinquish your joy of cooking just because one person is a better chef than the other. It's not fun being the one who does the dishes every time."*
—*Shauna*

FAVORITE THING IN THE KITCHEN: *"An electric juicer, for making fresh vegetable juice and sauces."*

—*Shauna and Dan*

PULLED PORK SANDWICHES

Serves 8

I came up with this recipe for a party at the Vashon Island home of my friend/food writer/best-selling author/all-around superwoman Shauna James Ahern and her husband, Danny. Shauna and her friends raved about it, and I hope you'll enjoy this simple recipe just as much! (Shauna has celiac disease and does not eat gluten, so she ate the pork without the bun. Some brands of ketchup, liquid smoke, and chicken stock contain trace amounts of gluten, so take care and research each ingredient if you are preparing this dish for a gluten-intolerant friend.) I like to serve this pulled pork piled high on toasted potato buns, with a side of blue cheese coleslaw.

$3^1/_2$ pounds boneless pork shoulder, cut into 4 equal pieces

1 cup ketchup

2 tablespoons molasses

$^2/_3$ cup apple cider vinegar

3 tablespoons Worcestershire sauce

3 tablespoons dark brown sugar

$^1/_3$ cup Dijon mustard

2 tablespoons liquid smoke

2 teaspoons garlic salt

$1^1/_4$ teaspoons freshly ground black pepper

2 tablespoons sweet paprika

$1^1/_2$ tablespoons ground cumin

2 teaspoons chili powder

$1^1/_4$ cups low-sodium chicken stock

8 of your favorite hamburger buns

1. Add all the ingredients, except for the hamburger buns, to a large stockpot. Simmer over medium-low heat for 3½ hours, partially uncovered, giving the pork a stir every hour or so to ensure it's not sticking to the bottom of the pot. Remove the meat from the sauce, and shred it with two forks (making sure to sneak a bite—it's so good!). Put the shredded meat back into the sauce and simmer over low heat, uncovered, for 30 to 45 minutes longer, or until the sauce reduces and thickens.

2. This pulled pork can be made up to 2 days ahead and refrigerated—in fact, the flavors get even better! Reheat it over medium heat for about 25 to 30 minutes, stirring often. Serve the pork piled on toasted, buttered hamburger buns, preferably with your favorite coleslaw.

BISTRO-STYLE FRENCH ONION SOUP

Serves 2

With a side salad and some baguette slices spread with good butter, this French onion soup makes for a simple, yet luxurious-tasting meal, ideal for cozying up together on a rainy day. Caramelizing the onions in the oven means less time spent stirring on the stove, and a touch of sherry vinegar really elevates the deep, rich flavors. This recipe contains a generous amount of cheese, because everyone knows that the blistered, golden brown layer of Gruyère is the very best part!

1 tablespoon extra-virgin olive oil

1 ounce slab bacon, cut into $^1/_2$-inch cubes

1 tablespoon unsalted butter

$^3/_4$ pound (about 2 large) yellow onions, thinly sliced

1 medium shallot, thinly sliced

2 small sprigs fresh thyme

1 bay leaf

3 cups beef stock or dark chicken stock, divided

3 tablespoons port wine

1 tablespoon sherry vinegar

Kosher salt and freshly ground black pepper

4 slices baguette

$3^1/_2$ ounces (about 1 cup) Gruyère, grated, divided

2 tablespoons grated Parmigiano-Reggiano, divided

1. Preheat the oven to 400°F.

2. Add the olive oil, bacon, butter, onions, shallots, thyme, and bay leaf to a heavy, ovenproof pot. Cover the pot tightly and place in the oven for 1 hour. Uncover the pot and stir the onions, then add $^1/_2$ cup of the stock. Cover the pot and place back in the oven for 1 hour, until the onions are soft and golden brown.

3. Remove the pot from the oven and place it on the stove top. Cook the onions over medium heat until they turn dark brown, 12 to 15 minutes, deglazing the pot with a few tablespoons of the stock if they begin to stick to the bottom. When the stock has evaporated, add the port wine and sherry vinegar, and stir until the liquids evaporate and reduce, about 3 minutes. (At this point, the onions should be very dark brown;

if not, cook them for another 5 minutes, scraping up the brown bits on the bottom of the pan and adding a touch more stock to keep them from sticking and burning.)

4. Add the remaining stock and increase the heat to high to bring the soup to a simmer. Decrease the heat to low once the soup is simmering, and cook, covered, for 30 minutes. Discard the bay leaf and thyme, and season to taste with salt and pepper.

5. Preheat the broiler.

6. Ladle the soup into two individual soup crocks. Top each crock with 2 slices of baguette, ½ cup of Gruyère, and 1 tablespoon of Parmigiano-Reggiano.

7. Broil the soup for about 4 minutes, keeping a close eye on the cheese so it doesn't burn. The soup is ready to eat once the cheese melts and turns golden brown.

A Roadside, Pork, and Bliss

❦

RYAN HARDY, EXECUTIVE CHEF OF MONTAGNA
AT THE LITTLE NELL IN ASPEN, COLORADO,
AND HIS WIFE, CATHY RUSNAK

Married: May 5, 2001

Often the best flavors and most romantic memories come at the most unexpected moments. Ryan Hardy, the executive chef at Montagna at The Little Nell in Aspen, Colorado, and his wife, Cathy Rusnak, were killing time at a Sunday flower market while visiting Pienza, Italy. Throughout the trip, Ryan had been on the lookout to try authentic Italian porchetta, and now Cathy spotted the object of his desire. The scene had all the right trappings—a butcher wielding a large knife over a whole filleted pig atop the porchetta stand—but this particular operation looked unappetizing to Ryan: a slab of plain meat shaved straight from the pig and plunked between two slices of crunchy, undressed white bread was surely not going to deliver the authentic porchetta experience he'd imagined. Nevertheless, at Cathy's urging, he reluctantly surrendered two euros, and the couple found a spot to squat on the side of the road and regard what looked like the homeliest sandwich they'd ever seen.

"We have these moments in life where you taste something and time just stands still," Ryan remembers. "This was one of those times. That sandwich was one of the most succulent, incredible food experiences I've ever had."

Nearly speechless, Ryan shoved the porchetta at Cathy, insisting she try it.

"It sounds ridiculous," Cathy concurs, "but it was absolute perfection."

"Here we are, sitting on an old curb, Fiats racing by at 60 miles an hour, and we are literally fighting over this sandwich," Ryan continues. "But how often do you get to share a wonderful piece of food, in a beautiful medieval town surrounded by florists, no less? I'll never forget it."

"And now Ryan has that porchetta on his menu," Cathy adds. "He brought that perfect experience we shared together back home to the restaurant."

"Food is romantic," Ryan states. "I've always felt so, and that is part of why I was drawn to this profession. This story is an example of how the simplest thing, when shared with someone you love, can be so memorable."

ADVICE FOR NEWLYWEDS: *"I find it's good for us if he does the cooking. I do the cleaning, and it's a perfect division of labor."*

—Cathy

"Shop seasonally. It's much more fun than people give credit for. Let the seasons guide you; wander through the store and create a meal from what you see. Instead of shopping to feed ourselves, we are shopping to feed our soul."

—Ryan

FAVORITE THINGS IN THE KITCHEN: *"A long time ago, Cathy discovered E. Dehillerin in Paris, which I now know is a famous cooking store. I bought three heirloom-quality copper pots and pans for a song, and I cook with them every single day. I absolutely cherish those pots."*

—Ryan

CUBAN ROAST SANDWICHES

Makes 6 large sandwiches

Paseo is a restaurant (or, more accurately, a tiny, tin-roofed shack) in Seattle with no signage. This no-frills Cuban spot has a line out the door every day, and most of the people are waiting to order the #2 Cuban Roast sandwich, voted by numerous magazines as one of the best sandwiches in America. The Cuban Roast is piled high with the juiciest, most tender pulled pork you've ever tasted, swathed in garlicky mayo and a generous heap of thickly sliced, caramelized onions. This recipe is a re-creation of that spectacular sandwich: give it a go, and make sure you both have a stack of napkins ready!

Begin marinating the pork a day before you plan to serve it. The garlic mayonnaise should also be prepared ahead as it needs to be refrigerated overnight.

FOR THE ROAST PORK:

$3\frac{1}{2}$ pounds bone-in pork shoulder, or 3 pounds boneless

10 cloves garlic, coarsely chopped

$1\frac{1}{2}$ tablespoons kosher salt

2 teaspoons freshly ground black pepper

2 cups orange juice

$\frac{1}{2}$ cup lime juice

2 tablespoons dark brown sugar

2 tablespoons chopped fresh oregano

$\frac{1}{2}$ cup extra-virgin olive oil

1 cup (about 1 large) diced onion

2 bay leaves

FOR THE GARLIC MAYONNAISE:

2 tablespoons finely minced garlic

$\frac{1}{4}$ teaspoon garlic salt

1 cup mayonnaise

3 tablespoons sweet relish

1 teaspoon freshly squeezed lemon juice

FOR THE SANDWICHES:

2 tablespoons extra-virgin olive oil

1 large yellow onion, cut into ¾-inch rings

Six 7-inch-long pieces baguette, split, toasted, and buttered

12 to 18 sprigs of cilantro

Pickled jalapeños

Romaine lettuce leaves

1. In a large resealable plastic bag, combine the pork, garlic, salt, pepper, orange juice, lime juice, brown sugar, oregano, olive oil, onion, and bay leaves. Seal the bag and place it in the refrigerator for at least 4 hours, preferably overnight.

2. To make the roast pork, preheat the oven to 300°F. Remove the pork from the bag, reserving the marinade, and place the pork in a roasting pan. Pour the reserved marinade (including the bay leaves) into the roasting pan, and tent the pan loosely with aluminum foil. Roast the pork, covered, for 2 hours on one side. Flip it over and roast, uncovered, on the other side for another 1½ to 2 hours, so the marinade has a chance to reduce slightly. After 3½ to 4 hours, the pork should be fall-off-the-bone tender—if not, roast it for another 15 minutes and check again.

3. Remove the pan from the oven and let the meat rest for 20 minutes, covered. Remove the foil and shred the pork into large chunks directly in the pan, mixing the remaining marinade into the meat to make it extra moist. The pork should be slightly pink from the ultraslow cooking time, and the juices should run clear. (The pork can be made a day ahead—simply reheat at 350°F for 30 minutes the next day.)

4. To make the garlic mayonnaise, combine all the ingredients in a small bowl, cover, and refrigerate overnight so the flavors meld together.

5. To assemble the sandwiches, heat the olive oil in a small skillet over medium-high heat for 1 minute. Add the sliced onions and sauté for about 4 minutes, until the edges of the onions just turn golden brown. (Alternatively, preheat the grill, toss the onions in the olive oil, and grill for 4 to 5 minutes, until the onions are lightly browned.)

6. Spoon a heaping tablespoon or two of the garlic mayonnaise on the top and bottom of the baguette pieces.

7. Layer a few cilantro leaves and jalapeño slices on the bottom of the baguette pieces, then pile on a generous amount of pork (¾ cup of meat is a good place to start). Top with the grilled onions and a few leaves of romaine, and then squish the top of the baguette down onto the sandwich.

MENU

A Summer Cookout

Sweet-and-Hot Chicken Kebabs, page 126

Pasta Salad with Arugula and Cherry Tomatoes, page 112

Cuban Roast Sandwiches, page 46

Strawberry Rhubarb Pie, page 208

The Morning After
SCONES, BISCUITS & OTHER BRUNCH GOODIES

Smoked Salmon Frittata

Blueberry Cinnamon Streusel Muffins

Turkey Sausage, Parmesan, and Artichoke Bake

Cheddar, Ham, and Dill Biscuits

Orange Blackberry Scones

Topsy-Turvy Apple French Toast

Chunky Monkey Banana Bread

Piña Colada Pancakes

Feathery Biscuits with Mushroom Thyme Gravy

Orange-Cinnamon Honey Sticky Buns

"DON'T SHOOT FOR THE MOON. LEARN TO MAKE ONE SIMPLE, NOURISHING RECIPE . . . SOON YOU'LL BE COMING UP WITH DISHES THAT ARE COMPLETELY YOUR OWN. EVENTUALLY, YOU'LL STOP FOLLOWING RECIPES AND START CREATING."

—*Neal Fraser, chef at BLD and Grace restaurants in Los Angeles, California*

SMOKED SALMON FRITTATA

Serves 2 to 4

The secret to this frittata is a bit of heavy cream—this extra ingredient helps keep the eggs delicate and silky, the way they're meant to be. I've taken the standard bagel toppings (smoked salmon, red onion, and cream cheese) and incorporated them into a frittata perfect for either breakfast or a light supper. With one person chopping the onions and the other beating the eggs and cream together, you'll have this on the table in minutes.

> **6 large eggs**
> **1/3 cup heavy cream**
> **1/4 teaspoon kosher salt**
> **1/4 teaspoon freshly ground black pepper**
> **2 tablespoons unsalted butter**
> **1/2 cup finely diced red onion**
> **1/2 cup (about 1 medium) thinly sliced leek, white and pale green**
>   **parts only**
> **4 ounces smoked salmon, cut into strips**
> **2 ounces goat cheese or cream cheese, cut into bite-size pieces**

1. Preheat the broiler.

2. In a large bowl, beat together the eggs, cream, salt, and pepper.

3. In a medium ovenproof skillet over medium heat, melt the butter. Add the onions and sauté for 10 to 12 minutes, or until they become soft and golden brown. Add the leeks and cook, stirring, for 3 minutes, until they are soft and tender. Lower the heat to low. Carefully pour the egg mixture on top, and gently stir the eggs for 30 seconds until they just begin to set. Allow the eggs to cook, undisturbed, for another 4 to 5 minutes, then lay the slices of salmon and goat cheese over the top.

4. Place the skillet in the oven and broil for 3 minutes, or until the top is lightly browned.

5. Slide the frittata onto a cutting board and cut into wedges before serving.

Scones, Biscuits & Other Brunch Goodies

BLUEBERRY CINNAMON STREUSEL MUFFINS

Makes 6 to 8 muffins

Blueberries, yogurt, and a softly spiced streusel topping make these muffins an irresistible part of any morning. If you have a few muffins left over, they freeze beautifully for up to two weeks. I always keep a few of these treats in my freezer and take them out the night before to defrost slowly for the next morning. A minute or two in the toaster oven, then split and buttered lavishly, and oh, what a breakfast! (Eating them together is mandatory; sharing with friends is optional.)

FOR THE MUFFINS:

$^1/_3$ cup vegetable oil, plus additional for greasing the muffin cups

$^2/_3$ cup sugar

1 large egg

$^2/_3$ cup plain yogurt

1 teaspoon (about 1 lemon or lime) freshly grated lemon or lime zest (optional)

$1^1/_2$ cups flour

$^1/_4$ teaspoon kosher salt

$1^1/_4$ teaspoons baking powder

$^1/_4$ teaspoon baking soda

$^1/_2$ teaspoon ground cinnamon

$^1/_4$ teaspoon ground nutmeg

$1^1/_4$ cups blueberries, divided

FOR THE STREUSEL:

3 tablespoons flour

$^1/_4$ cup oatmeal

3 tablespoons dark brown sugar

$^1/_4$ teaspoon ground cinnamon

2 tablespoons unsalted butter, cut into $^1/_4$-inch cubes

1. Preheat the oven to 375°F.

2. To make the muffins, lightly grease the muffin cups with vegetable oil and set aside.

3. In a large bowl, stir together the vegetable oil, sugar, egg, yogurt, and lemon zest. In another bowl, stir together the flour, salt, baking powder, baking soda, cinnamon, and nutmeg. Add the dry ingredients to the wet ingredients, and mix lightly until just combined, taking care not to overmix (the batter should be slightly lumpy). Fold half the blueberries into the batter and fill the prepared muffin cups almost to the top. Divide the remaining blueberries, placing a few on top of each muffin.

4. To make the streusel, in a medium bowl combine the flour, oatmeal, brown sugar, and cinnamon. Cut the butter in with a pastry blender or two knives until the mixture resembles coarse crumbs.

5. Sprinkle some streusel on top of each muffin. Bake the muffins for 25 to 30 minutes, or until a toothpick inserted in the center of one of the muffins comes out clean.

A Peasant Tradition

❧

MATTHEW WEINGARTEN, EXECUTIVE CHEF
AT INSIDE PARK AT ST. BART'S IN NEW YORK
CITY, AND HIS WIFE, KATKA PETRIKOVA

Married: August 18, 2001

Matthew Weingarten wasn't seeking out another member of the food community when he was looking for a girlfriend. Katka Petrikova appealed to him because she had little interest in New York's restaurant world but possessed a deep appreciation for culture and history, as well as food. The pair bonded over huge bowls of borscht and loaves of challah bread at an Eastern European dive in the East Village, sharing memories about her Slovakian background and his Jewish childhood. After they fell in love, Katka would often wait up for him, cooking midnight meals of casseroles and one-pot dishes she remembered from her past.

"Those simple, hearty dishes were truly extraordinary," Matt says. "The more she cooked like that, the more her style worked into my repertoire."

The most profound influence came when Matt and Katka journeyed to Slovakia to meet her family. Watching Katka's mother cook and observing her use of seasonal ingredients and preserves, Matt began to think differently about food. He found himself tapping into his own memories and longing to re-create the dissolving culinary traditions of his past.

At Katka's grandparents' house, Matt sat with Katka's grandfather, sharing a simple meal of fresh pork sausage, pickled pearl onions, and plum brandy—all of which were made from scratch—and had a revelation.

"I told myself, 'This is what I want to do, to focus on these heritage foods and keep these ancient traditions alive,'" Matt remembers thinking.

He did just that, working old-world traditions into his kitchen repertoire and introducing in-house pickling, canning, preserving, and baking, as well as homemade cheese and charcuterie to the menu. Matt admits to "somewhat fancifying" the farm-to-table peasant food for New Yorkers, but says he gets so much joy creating dishes that are essentially Katka's. "She can recognize the dumplings I had at her grandmother's house on the menu," Matt says. "It makes us happy."

Of all that he's learned, nothing is more amusing to Matt than the fact that the one person with whom he never expected to share his culinary world has had more influence on his cooking than anyone else.

"I would not be successful without her," Matt says firmly. "Maybe I would have found a different focus, but I don't believe it would be as good. I'm working our personal heritages into my dishes, and that makes them so much more meaningful and beautiful."

ADVICE FOR NEWLYWEDS: *"The most amazing gift you can give your spouse or children is to cook something your mother or grandparents cooked for you that was your favorite thing as a child."*

—Matt

FAVORITE THING IN THE KITCHEN: *"We have a great little wooden spoon for scraping up sauces and stirring everything—it's all we need."*

—Matt

TURKEY SAUSAGE, PARMESAN, AND ARTICHOKE BAKE

Serves 2

I love a savory breakfast, and this one will get you both off on the right foot, with a balanced combination of lean turkey sausage, eggs, and vegetables. The best part is you can throw everything together the night before, place the little individual casseroles in the refrigerator, and then just put them directly into the oven the next morning for a hot, satisfying breakfast that won't leave either of you running late for work.

1 tablespoon extra-virgin olive oil

6 ounces turkey sausage, casings removed

$1/2$ cup finely diced sweet yellow onion

2 large eggs

$2/3$ cup whole milk (or half-and-half, if you're feeling decadent)

$1/2$ cup grated Parmesan

$1/2$ teaspoon chopped fresh thyme

$1/4$ teaspoon kosher salt

$1/8$ teaspoon freshly ground black pepper

$1/2$ cup diced marinated artichoke hearts

2 cups cubed day-old bread

4 thin slices tomato

4 fresh basil leaves

$1/3$ cup grated mozzarella cheese

1. Preheat the oven to 350°F.

2. Heat the olive oil in a medium skillet over medium-high heat. Add the sausage and onions and cook for 4 to 5 minutes, breaking up the sausage with your spatula, until the onions are soft and the sausage is browned. Remove from the heat (the sausage will finish cooking in the oven).

3. In a large bowl, beat together the eggs, milk, Parmesan, thyme, salt, and pepper. Stir in the sausage mixture, artichokes, and bread cubes.

4. Ladle the mixture into individual ramekins (or a small casserole dish). Top with the tomato slices, basil leaves, and mozzarella. (If you want to bake these the next morning, just cover the ramekins with plastic wrap and place them in the refrigerator.)

5. Bake for 25 to 30 minutes, or until the casseroles are puffed and golden.

CHEDDAR, HAM, AND DILL BISCUITS

Makes eight 2½-inch biscuits

These biscuits bake up supremely tender and moist with a tiny bit of cornstarch and tangy buttermilk mixed into the dough. Flecked with cheese, ham, and herbs, they are a delicious, savory breakfast treat any day of the week. I like to break them apart and slather them with lots of butter. If you don't like the taste of dill, fresh chives would make a lovely substitute.

2 cups flour

2 tablespoons cornstarch

1 tablespoon baking powder

¼ teaspoon baking soda

1 tablespoon sugar

1 teaspoon kosher salt

½ teaspoon freshly ground black pepper

½ cup (1 stick) cold unsalted butter, cut into ¼-inch cubes

¾ cup packed shredded sharp cheddar

1 cup diced ham

3 tablespoons chopped fresh dill

⅔ cup buttermilk

1 egg yolk

2 tablespoons whole milk

1. Preheat the oven to 425°F.

2. In a large bowl, stir together the flour, cornstarch, baking powder, baking soda, sugar, salt, and pepper. Cut the butter into the flour with a pastry blender or two knives until the mixture resembles coarse crumbs. Add the cheddar, ham, and dill, and stir in the buttermilk until just combined. (Take care not to overmix, or your biscuits will be tough.)

CHEDDAR, HAM, AND
DILL BISCUITS

3. In a small bowl, add the egg yolk and milk and whisk to combine.

4. Turn the dough out onto a lightly floured surface and pat into a rectangle about
    $1\frac{1}{2}$ inches thick. Cut 8 biscuits with a floured $2\frac{1}{2}$-inch biscuit cutter (or a glass of
    about the same diameter, turned upside down) and place on a parchment- or
    Silpat-lined baking sheet. Lightly brush the top of each biscuit with a bit of the
    beaten egg yolk mixture.

5. Bake the biscuits for 15 minutes, or until they are golden brown. Enjoy them when
    they're hot out of the oven.

For the Love of Cooking

AMY AND NEAL FRASER, CHEF-OWNERS
AT BLD AND GRACE RESTAURANTS
IN LOS ANGELES, CALIFORNIA

Married: May 25, 2003

The very genesis of BLD, Amy and Neal Fraser's second Los Angeles restaurant, epitomizes what the couple values most about food: comfort and love. After Amy became pregnant in 2005, she found that fueling her body with breakfast was essential. Neal quickly stepped in, creating memorable, heaping plates of food that made Amy swoon with happiness. Most of his dishes came from whatever was left over in the family refrigerator: eggs scrambled with chorizo, *piquillo* peppers, *lomo curado* (Spanish dry-cured pork tenderloin), and smoked paprika was a favorite, as were pillowy blueberry ricotta pancakes.

"It was food with love in it," Amy says. "Everything he cooked for me when I was pregnant was so comforting and wholesome. We had never really done breakfast together before, but he knew exactly what I wanted and needed."

The couple was disappointed, though, when they ventured out in search of like-minded food in the restaurants of their Fairfax neighborhood. They found good food in unsavory environments, bad food in stuffy surroundings, and aloof waitstaff nearly everywhere. "We wanted to find a clean, comfortable place that graciously served 'food made from home' kind of food," Amy says. "Food simply made and served with love."

Thus, BLD—short for Breakfast, Lunch, Dinner—was born, with the idea of combining all of those nurturing elements under one roof.

"It's just like home cooking," Neal says. "If you have all the right components, your food will always taste good." Successful cooking at the Fraser household, Neal continues, is as simple as bringing home two dozen oysters, sprinkling them with sherry wine vinegar, throwing in some chopped shallots, and sharing them with Amy. "Keep it simple. Buy the best product you can afford and treat it with respect. Salt and pepper go a long way."

As for Amy, the experience of launching BLD inspired her to teach herself to cook. A dedicated recipe follower, she is slowly learning to craft the same simple dishes Neal made during her pregnancy, such as lasagna and roast chicken.

"I decided that I couldn't be offended by anyone's opinion until I was good at it," Amy says. "I ask for as much feedback as possible. Now Neal enjoys my cooking, and that makes me feel great."

ADVICE FOR NEWLYWEDS: *"Follow the same process every time. You can't put your pants on and then your underwear and not have people look at you weird, but people do that all the time with cooking."*

—Neal

FAVORITE THING IN THE KITCHEN: *"My Staub cast-iron pan. It's good for everything, from scrambling eggs to braising meat."*

—Neal

ORANGE BLACKBERRY SCONES

Makes 8 scones

It might be a cliché, but it's true: the very best way to start off any lazy weekend morning together is with a pot of coffee, a couple of scones, and a shared newspaper. These scones are perfect vehicles for clotted cream and generous dollops of lemon curd. They are also wonderful with melted butter.

> **2 cups flour, sifted**
> **$^1/_2$ cup sugar**
> **1 tablespoon baking powder**
> **$^1/_2$ teaspoon kosher salt**
> **2 teaspoons (about $^1/_2$ medium orange) freshly grated orange zest**
> **$^1/_2$ cup (1 stick) cold unsalted butter, cut into $^1/_4$-inch cubes**
> **$^3/_4$ cup heavy cream, plus 1 to 2 tablespoons extra, if needed**
> **1 cup blackberries**
> **1 egg yolk**
> **2 tablespoons whole milk**

1. Preheat the oven to 425°F.

2. In a large bowl, stir together the flour, sugar, baking powder, salt, and orange zest. Cut the butter into the flour mixture with a pastry blender or two knives until the mixture resembles coarse crumbs. Stir in the heavy cream until just combined. (If the mixture is a little too dry and won't hold together, stir in the extra cream.) Fold in the blackberries.

3. In a small bowl, add the egg yolk and milk and whisk to combine.

4. Gently turn the dough out onto a lightly floured surface and shape it into a circle about 8 inches in diameter. Cut the dough in half, and then cut each half into 4 wedges. Place the scones on a parchment- or Silpat-lined baking sheet and brush each with a bit of the beaten egg yolk mixture.

5. Bake the scones for 15 to 18 minutes, or until they are golden brown. These scones are best enjoyed when they're hot out of the oven.

TOPSY-TURVY APPLE FRENCH TOAST

Serves 2 to 4

When you have a few friends coming over for brunch, wouldn't you rather be toasting to your newlywed status over mimosas instead of flipping batches of French toast on the stove? This upside-down French toast is baked in the oven, so no one needs to be relegated to kitchen duties. The dish comes out of the oven with a crown of cinnamony, brown sugar–baked apples on top—pretty enough to serve on that newly acquired wedding china. In the summertime, why not substitute fresh peaches for the apples? To really gild the lily, try serving each wedge with a scoop of ice cream.

4 tablespoons (1/2 stick) unsalted butter, plus extra for greasing the pan

2 Granny Smith apples, peeled, cored, and cut into 1/4-inch slices

1/4 cup plus 1 tablespoon packed dark brown sugar

1 tablespoon ground cinnamon

1/2 teaspoon ground nutmeg

1/2 teaspoon kosher salt

1/4 cup heavy cream

3 large eggs

3/4 cup whole milk

1 tablespoon vanilla extract

6 slices white bread (or substitute challah for a richer taste)

1/4 cup raisins (optional)

1/4 cup coarsely chopped walnuts (optional)

1. Preheat the oven to 350°F. Grease a 9-inch cake pan with butter and set aside.

2. In a medium skillet, melt the butter over medium heat. Add the apple slices, brown sugar, cinnamon, nutmeg, salt, and cream. Cook until the cream reduces slightly and the apples are slightly softened, about 5 to 6 minutes.

3. In a bowl large enough to hold the bread, stir together the eggs, milk, and vanilla. Soak the bread in the egg mixture until the bread has thoroughly absorbed the liquid, about 5 minutes.

4. In the prepared pan, arrange the apple slices concentrically, slightly overlapping one another. Spoon any of the leftover sauce from the pan over the apples. Sprinkle the raisins and walnuts over the apples, then lay the bread over the apples, pressing down so the slices lay fairly even. Pour any leftover milk onto the bread.

5. Bake for 35 minutes, or until the bread is puffed and golden. Run a knife along the edge of the French toast to loosen, then place a large plate or cake platter directly on top of the pan. Flip them both over in one motion and slide the pan off. Cut into wedges and serve plain, dusted with icing sugar, or with ice cream.

CHUNKY MONKEY BANANA BREAD

Makes one 9-by-5-inch loaf

The secret to this time-honored banana bread is sour cream, an ingredient that renders many baked goods incomparably moist. This version combines sour cream with walnuts, chocolate chips, and a bit of sweet cinnamon heat for a loaf pretty enough to serve as dessert, with a dab of cardamom-scented whipped cream. Of course, it's also a fantastic treat to share just plain, with melted butter and a cup of afternoon tea.

2 cups flour
3/4 teaspoon kosher salt
1/2 teaspoon baking soda
1 teaspoon baking powder
1 teaspoon ground cinnamon
1/2 cup (1 stick) unsalted butter, softened
3/4 cup light brown sugar
3/4 cup granulated sugar
2 teaspoons vanilla extract
1 1/2 cups (about 3 large) mashed overripe bananas
1 cup full-fat sour cream
2 large eggs
1/2 cup chopped walnuts
1/2 cup semisweet chocolate chips

1. Preheat the oven to 350°F. Grease and line a 9-by-5-inch loaf pan with parchment paper cut to fit the bottom of the pan.

2. In a medium bowl, stir together the flour, salt, baking soda, baking powder, and cinnamon.

3. In a large bowl, with an electric mixer on medium speed, cream together the butter, brown sugar, and granulated sugar for 3 to 4 minutes, until the butter mixture becomes light and fluffy. Beat in the vanilla, bananas, sour cream, and eggs.

4. Stir in the dry ingredients with a wooden spoon, then stir in the walnuts and chocolate chips. Pour the batter into the prepared pan and bake for 60 to 65 minutes, or until a toothpick inserted in the center of the loaf comes out clean. Let the loaf cool for 10 minutes in the pan before carefully turning it out onto a wire rack, discarding the parchment paper.

Scones, Biscuits & Other Brunch Goodies

The Family That Eats Together, Stays Together

❧❦❧

LISA DUPAR AND JONATHAN ZIMMER, CHEF-OWNERS
OF LISA DUPAR CATERING AND POMEGRANATE
BISTRO IN REDMOND, WASHINGTON

Married: September 9, 2001

T he kitchen is our place of peace," says Lisa Dupar with convic-
tion. "At work we are focused and have our roles, but at home it's
fun and playful." Both she and her husband, Jonathan Zimmer,
are chefs at the catering business and restaurant they own together. Once
home, they check their egos at the kitchen door and consistently express
gratitude when one cooks for the other.

"Fighting about food is no fun," Lisa says. "We're just thankful to get
dinner on the table, and we always make sure to say so."

The couple each had two children when they married and lean on the
comfort and consistency of traditions—upholding established ones as
well as creating new ones—to keep the family harmonious. A few years ago
they began celebrating their kids' birthdays with "dream dinners," small,
sky's-the-limit dinner parties for the guest of honor with his or her best
friends.

"We value getting together more than anything else," Jonathan says,
"so we thought, 'Let's treat them to what we do best and have them choose
the menu.'" For Lisa and Jonathan's kids, who are all in their twenties,
that might mean plates of foie gras, oysters on the half shell, marinated
lamb chops, and treasured wines pulled from the couple's collection.

Likewise, they pull out all the stops for major holidays. At Christ-
mastime, Lisa revisits her Southern roots and cooks oyster stew, while
Jonathan rises early to make homemade cinnamon rolls, sticky buns, or
scones.

"It doesn't matter how old they are," Jonathan says. "Kids like to eat
food that brings back happy memories. My daughter still says that nobody

makes scones like the ones I baked for her when she was young." For that reason, Jonathan and Lisa always make the same Thanksgiving menu, swapping out only sweet and savory pie flavors from year to year. "There are so many emotional feelings that come with food," Jonathan says. "You bring back memories every time you sit down with what is familiar."

ADVICE FOR NEWLYWEDS: *"If your spouse is going to make soup and you felt like having a steak, let it go and just be thankful they're cooking for you. Always appreciate someone doing work for you—even if it's the work you love to do best."*

—Lisa

"Find common ground in the kitchen. Pick the thing you like to do and know that everything from prep to cleanup is contributing to the cooking process."

—Jonathan

FAVORITE THINGS IN THE KITCHEN: *"A great set of cutting boards in many sizes, lots of good olive oils and vinegars, and a collection of herb plants."*

—Lisa and Jonathan

PIÑA COLADA PANCAKES

Makes about 6 pancakes

This pancake recipe yields the softest, most tender pancakes I've ever eaten. Each bite is a bit of pillowy heaven, thanks to the buttermilk and a good amount of leavening. Pour on the hot, rummy coconut syrup with a lavish hand, saving at least a *few* sinful drops for your sweetie.

1 cup flour
2 tablespoons sugar
2 teaspoons baking powder
$1/2$ teaspoon baking soda
$1/8$ teaspoon kosher salt
2 large eggs
2 tablespoons unsalted butter, melted
2 teaspoons coconut extract
$2/3$ cup buttermilk
$1/2$ cup crushed pineapple, drained, juices reserved
Vegetable oil for cooking the pancakes
Whipped cream, for garnish
$1/4$ cup toasted sweetened, flaked coconut, for garnish
Buttered Coconut Rum Syrup (recipe follows)

1. In a large bowl, stir together the flour, sugar, baking powder, baking soda, and salt.

2. In a separate bowl, stir together the eggs, melted butter, coconut extract, buttermilk, and the drained pineapple. Make a well in the dry ingredients and pour the wet ingredients into the center. Mix lightly until just combined, taking care not to overmix (the batter should be slightly lumpy).

3. Grease a large skillet or griddle lightly with vegetable oil, and turn the heat on medium. Ladle about $1/2$ cup of batter for each pancake. (To speed up the process, have two skillets side by side on the stove, so you can whip up several pancakes at once.) Cook the pancakes for several minutes on the first side, flipping when the surface is covered in bubbles. Cook the other side for another minute or two, and repeat with the remaining batter.

4. To serve, stack as many pancakes as your stomachs can hold and top generously with the warm Buttered Coconut Rum Syrup. Garnish with whipped cream and toasted coconut for an extra-special brunch.

PIÑA COLADA
PANCAKES

BUTTERED COCONUT RUM SYRUP

Makes about 1½ cups of syrup

> **2 teaspoons cornstarch**
> **2 tablespoons water**
> **½ cup packed dark brown sugar**
> **3 tablespoons unsalted butter**
> **¾ cup coconut cream**
> **1½ tablespoons light rum**
> **2 tablespoons pineapple juice**
> **Small pinch of kosher salt**

1. In a small bowl, dissolve the cornstarch in the water and set aside. Combine all the other ingredients in a small saucepan, and stir over medium heat until the syrup starts to steam. Add the cornstarch slurry all at once, and stir until the mixture bubbles.

FEATHERY BISCUITS WITH MUSHROOM THYME GRAVY

Makes eight 2½-inch biscuits

The mere promise of fluffy, tender-crumbed biscuits, split open and blanketed with creamy mushroom thyme gravy, is sure to nudge your beloved sleepyhead out of bed. Try topping each biscuit with a soft-yolked egg and have a platter of crispy, salty bacon waiting on the table for a truly sublime way to start your weekend together.

> 2 cups flour, sifted
> 3 teaspoons baking powder
> ½ teaspoon baking soda
> ¾ teaspoon kosher salt
> 4 tablespoons (½ stick) cold unsalted butter
> ¼ cup cold lard or shortening
> ¾ cup buttermilk
> 1 egg yolk
> 2 tablespoons whole milk
> Mushroom Thyme Gravy (recipe follows)

1. Preheat the oven to 425°F.

2. In a large bowl, stir together the flour, baking powder, baking soda, and salt. Add the butter and lard, and cut in with a pastry blender (or two knives) until the mixture resembles coarse, pea-size lumps. Stir in the buttermilk, taking care not to overmix, or your biscuits will be tough.

3. In a small bowl, add the egg yolk and milk and whisk to combine.

4. Turn the dough out onto a lightly floured surface and knead it a couple of times, just until it comes together. With a floured rolling pin, roll the dough to a thickness of 1 inch, then cut out eight biscuits with a 2½-inch floured biscuit cutter (or a glass of about the same diameter, turned upside down). Place the biscuits on a parchment- or Silpat-lined cookie sheet, and lightly brush the top of each one with a bit of the beaten egg yolk mixture.

5. Bake the biscuits for 12 to 15 minutes, or until they are golden brown and nicely risen. Ladle the Mushroom Thyme Gravy over the hot biscuits and dive in!

MUSHROOM THYME GRAVY

Makes about 3 cups of gravy

> 6 tablespoons unsalted butter
> 1 cup (about 1 medium) finely diced sweet yellow onion
> 7 ounces (about 2½ cups) cremini mushrooms, diced
> ¼ cup flour
> 2 cups half-and-half
> 1 teaspoon chopped fresh thyme
> Kosher salt
> Red pepper flakes

1. In a large skillet, melt the butter over medium-high heat. Add the onions and cook until caramelized, 7 to 8 minutes. Add the mushrooms and cook until the mushrooms are soft, 2 to 3 minutes. Add the flour and stir for another minute. Pour in the half-and-half and add the thyme, stirring until the gravy bubbles and thickens, about 3 to 4 minutes. Season with salt and red pepper flakes to taste.

ORANGE-CINNAMON HONEY STICKY BUNS

Makes 14 sticky buns

I know I shouldn't play favorites, but if I had to pick one recipe to make from the brunch section of this cookbook, this would be it. The best part about these buns is they contain a lot less sugar than most sticky bun recipes, so they're not cloyingly sweet. Most of the work is done the night before, so in the morning, all you have to do is pop the pan in the oven. It takes a little love and elbow grease, but the results are heavenly.

FOR THE DOUGH:

    7 tablespoons unsalted butter at room temperature, plus
       1 tablespoon for greasing the bowl
    $1/4$ cup warm water (105°F to 115°F)
    3 teaspoons instant dry yeast
    $1/3$ cup sugar, divided
    $1^1/4$ teaspoons kosher salt
    1 large egg, slightly beaten
    1 egg yolk
    2 heaping tablespoons (about 1 medium orange) freshly grated
       orange zest
    1 cup whole milk or buttermilk, at room temperature
    $4^1/4$ cups flour, divided

FOR THE FILLING:

    4 tablespoons ($1/2$ stick) unsalted butter, melted and cooled
    $2/3$ cup packed light brown sugar
    3 teaspoons ground cinnamon

FOR THE GLAZE:

    $1/2$ cup (1 stick) unsalted butter
    $3/4$ cup packed light brown sugar
    $1/4$ cup honey
    $1/4$ cup heavy cream
    $1^1/2$ cups chopped pecans or walnuts
    2 teaspoons (about $1/2$ medium orange) freshly grated orange zest
    3 tablespoons freshly squeezed orange juice
    $1/4$ teaspoon kosher salt

ORANGE-CINNAMON
HONEY STICKY BUNS

1. To make the dough, lightly grease a large bowl with 1 tablespoon of the butter and set aside. In the bowl of a stand mixer combine the water, yeast, and 1 teaspoon of the sugar. Stir to dissolve and let stand until foamy (about 5 minutes.)

2. Add the remaining sugar, the salt, the remaining butter, egg, egg yolk, orange zest, milk, and 3 cups of the flour. Mix on low speed until combined. Switch to a dough hook and continue mixing on low speed, slowly adding the remaining flour $\frac{1}{4}$ cup at a time. Increase the speed to medium and mix until the dough looks silky smooth and a bit tacky, but not too sticky. (If the dough is too wet, add another tablespoon or two of flour.) Continue mixing for 3 to 4 minutes. Turn the mixer off, and shape the dough into a ball.

3. Put the dough in the greased bowl, turning it so that it is completely covered in butter. Lay a sheet of plastic wrap directly on the surface of the dough, patting it down lightly around the edge of the bowl so that the dough is not exposed to too much air. Let the dough rise in a warm spot until it doubles in volume (about 2 hours). After the dough has risen, punch it down, discard the plastic wrap, and turn it out onto a lightly floured surface.

4. With a floured rolling pin, roll the dough into a rectangle measuring 18 by 9 inches. To make the filling, brush the dough with the melted butter and sprinkle evenly with the brown sugar and cinnamon. Roll up the dough from one long end, so it forms a cigar-shaped, cinnamon-spiral log. Arrange the log so it rests seam side down, then slice it into 14 equal pieces.

5. To make the glaze, combine all the ingredients in a small saucepan and heat, stirring, just until melted. Pour the glaze into a $13\frac{3}{4}$-by-$9\frac{3}{4}$-inch baking pan. Arrange the sticky buns in the pan (there should be a little bit of room for them to rise). Cover the pan with plastic wrap, and place in the refrigerator overnight.

6. The next morning, preheat the oven to 350°F. Remove the plastic wrap from the pan, and bake the sticky buns for 25 to 30 minutes, or until they are golden brown.

7. Let the buns cool for 5 to 10 minutes before turning them out onto a large baking sheet. Let them cool for another 10 minutes before serving.

Sunday Brunch Is Served

Cheddar, Ham, and Dill Biscuits, page 57

Turkey Sausage, Parmesan, and Artichoke Bake, page 56

Orange-Cinnamon Honey Sticky Buns, page 73

Who Gets the Remote?
COMFORTING MEALS
FOR LAZY NIGHTS

My Award-Winning Four-Cheese Mac-and-Cheese

Creamy Kale Gratin

Creamy Langoustine Pasta with Fresh Tomato Sauce

Taiwanese Beef Noodle Soup

Slow-Cooked Lamb Ragù

Red Wine and Mushroom Risotto

"I DON'T WANT TO GO OUT AND BE SOCIAL. I JUST
WANT TO STAY IN AND COOK AND HANG WITH HIM."

—*Kimberly Paley, co-owner, Paley's Place in Portland, Oregon, on Vitaly, her husband of 21 years*

MY AWARD-WINNING FOUR-CHEESE MAC-AND-CHEESE

Serves 2 to 4

This recipe is incredibly dear to me, because it was my first award-winning dish. A couple of years ago, over a hundred people in Seattle attended a charity event in which sixteen chefs competed against one another for the title of "Best Mac-and-Cheese." Being by far the youngest and least experienced entrant, I was overjoyed when I won. This mac-and-cheese is packed with bacon, fresh herbs, a blend of four cheeses, and a crispy crumb topping. I hope this is a dish you'll both share as often as my husband and I do.

1 tablespoon vegetable oil

4 strips bacon, cut into 1/4-inch pieces

3 tablespoons unsalted butter, divided

3/4 cup (about 1 medium) finely chopped sweet yellow onion

2 tablespoons flour

3 tablespoons dry white wine

1 1/4 cups half-and-half

1 1/2 teaspoons dried marjoram (or 3/4 teaspoon chopped fresh marjoram)

3/4 teaspoon chopped fresh thyme

Pinch of red pepper flakes

1/2 teaspoon freshly ground black pepper

1/4 pound fresh, whole-milk mozzarella, cubed

1/4 pound blue cheese (such as Stilton or Roquefort), crumbled

1/4 pound Parmigiano-Reggiano, grated

1/4 pound Gruyère, grated

Kosher salt

1/2 pound pasta, cooked, drained, and kept hot

1/2 cup panko (or substitute regular bread crumbs)

Chives or parsley, for garnish (optional)

1. Heat the oil in a large skillet over medium-high heat. Add the bacon and cook until crisp, about 3 to 4 minutes. Remove the bacon with a slotted spoon and place on paper towels to drain, reserving the drippings in the pan. Add 2 tablespoons of the butter to the skillet, then add the onions and sauté for 7 to 8 minutes, or until they are golden brown. Stir in the flour and the wine, and cook for 2 minutes. Add the half-and-half, marjoram, thyme, red pepper flakes, pepper, mozzarella, blue cheese, Parmigiano-Reggiano, and Gruyère. Stir until the cheeses melt into the cream sauce and the sauce begins to bubble and thicken. Taste the sauce and if necessary, season with the salt. Add the cooked pasta, mixing thoroughly to coat with the sauce.

2. In a small skillet, toast the panko with the remaining butter until it is golden brown and crisp. Season with a tiny pinch of pepper and salt, if desired.

3. Spoon the pasta into big bowls and top with a generous amount of panko and a sprinkle of bacon. Garnish with a few snipped chives, if desired.

A Saveur *Sequel*

❧

CYNTHIA NIMS, AUTHOR OF TWELVE
COOKBOOKS, AND HER HUSBAND, BOB BURNS

Married: March 20, 1993

When Cynthia Nims and Bob Burns joke that Bob only cooks about once a decade, it's no exaggeration. The couple had only dated a few times when Bob decided to treat his new girlfriend to dinner at his bachelor pad. "I invited her over and figured she could watch me cook, and the effort would earn me some points," Bob remembers, before deadpanning: "It didn't."

For the apple of his eye—a lifelong gourmand who would soon leave to study cooking at École de Cuisine La Varenne in France—Bob heated up ready-to-eat garlic bread and a jar of pasta sauce to which he added watery canned mushrooms. He served "a reasonably fresh salad" with tomatoes and bottled salad dressing, and boiled not only the spaghetti but also the broccoli, which Cynthia describes as being so overcooked that it turned from green to pale yellow. There was no dessert.

"It was a nice gesture and I appreciated it, and in retrospect I was probably too critical of his cooking," Cynthia concedes. "But, oh yuck, canned mushrooms!"

As for Bob, he admits that he learned a valuable lesson that night: "I should not cook again for this woman until I knew what I was doing."

So six years later, Bob invited her again for dinner. When she arrived, he greeted her in a pressed white shirt, tie, and apron. "Welcome to Chez Bob," he announced gallantly and led her into a clean apartment with a properly set table. This time, the vinaigrette was homemade, and the mushrooms were fresh. He lightly steamed the broccoli and made his own garlic butter spread atop a fresh baguette. And this time, there was dessert: a diamond engagement ring and a formal proposal down on one knee.

"It was so sweet for him to re-create the very first meal he ever made me—but properly," says Cynthia, who, on that night, spoke only in the affirmative.

As for Chez Bob, it was open for one night only, though the self-proclaimed "foodie spouse" will occasionally perform as sous-chef "under extreme circumstances."

"We have a really great partnership in that I do all of the cooking and he does all of the cleanup—and the eating, of course," Cynthia laughs. "Food is such an integral part of life. The trick is finding what makes you the happiest as a couple and making the most of that."

ADVICE FOR NEWLYWEDS: *"Once you move in together, the kitchen dynamic changes. Sometimes harmony means taking direction and not taking it personally."*

—*Bob*

"Figure out what your meal-sharing comfort will be. Sometimes one person is the chef and the other is the eater. It's not the same for everybody."

—*Cynthia*

FAVORITE THING IN THE KITCHEN: *"Paper towels! They're useful dry and damp for wrapping fresh herbs and lettuce, topping bowls of prepped items, and lying flat under a chopping board to keep it from slipping."*

—*Cynthia*

CREAMY KALE GRATIN

Serves 8 as a side dish

A darling little French restaurant in Seattle called Boat Street Cafe serves a creamy kale gratin topped with lush slices of melty mozzarella that is positively swoon-worthy. That incredible dish inspired this recipe, which is perfect as a comforting side for a night in as well as for passing around the holiday table.

> 2 tablespoons extra-virgin olive oil
>
> 1 large sweet yellow onion, finely chopped
>
> 3 bunches kale and/or Swiss chard, ribs discarded, leaves roughly chopped 1 inch thick
>
> 3 cloves garlic, finely chopped
>
> 2 teaspoons kosher salt
>
> $^3/_4$ teaspoon freshly ground black pepper
>
> Pinch of red pepper flakes (optional)
>
> $^1/_2$ teaspoon ground nutmeg
>
> 7 tablespoons unsalted butter
>
> 7 tablespoons flour
>
> 1$^1/_4$ cups whole milk
>
> 2 cups heavy cream
>
> 8 ounces fresh whole-milk mozzarella, cut into $^1/_4$-inch slices

1. Preheat the oven to 350°F.

2. Heat the olive oil in a large skillet over medium-high heat. Add the onions and sauté until caramelized, about 7 to 8 minutes. Add the kale several handfuls at a time, waiting for it to wilt a bit before fitting more into the pan. Add the garlic and cook for 4 to 5 minutes, or until the kale is wilted and tender. Add the salt, pepper, red pepper flakes, and nutmeg. Transfer the kale mixture to a colander and drain any excess liquid. Put the drained kale into a large bowl.

3. In a medium saucepan, melt the butter over medium heat. Add the flour and stir using a whisk, cooking out the raw flour taste, for 1 to 2 minutes. Add the milk and cream, stirring continuously, until the cream mixture is smooth and bubbly and has thickened. Remove from the heat and pour the hot cream mixture over the kale. Mix thoroughly and pour the kale mixture into a large casserole pan. Distribute the mozzarella slices evenly over the top.

4. Bake for 30 to 35 minutes on the top rack of the oven, until the cheese is melted and golden brown. Let cool for 5 to 10 minutes before serving.

CREAMY LANGOUSTINE PASTA WITH FRESH TOMATO SAUCE

Serves 2

Langoustines are some of my favorite shellfish. They are sweeter than shrimp or prawns, but you can substitute either of those in this recipe if they're not available in your area. The secret to this pasta is using a skillet to cook the sauce—the larger surface area allows the sauce to reduce quickly, for a long-simmered taste in a fraction of the time. Pair this with your favorite white wine and clink your glasses to a couple's night in.

2 tablespoons unsalted butter

$^1/_2$ cup (about 2 medium) finely diced shallots

2 cloves garlic, finely chopped

1 teaspoon chopped fresh oregano

One 14.5-ounce can diced tomatoes

Pinch of red pepper flakes (optional)

$^3/_4$ teaspoon kosher salt

$^1/_2$ teaspoon freshly ground black pepper

1 cup halved cherry tomatoes

3 tablespoons dry white wine

$^1/_4$ cup heavy cream

$^1/_2$ pound langoustine tails or shrimp, peeled and deveined, defrosted if frozen

$^1/_4$ cup fresh basil, roughly torn (optional)

$^1/_2$ pound pasta, cooked and drained

1. In a large skillet over medium heat, melt the butter. Add the shallots and sauté for 7 to 8 minutes, or until they are golden brown. Add the garlic, oregano, canned tomatoes, red pepper flakes, salt, and pepper. Then add the cherry tomatoes, wine, and heavy cream. Increase the heat to medium-high and cook the sauce for 5 to 6 minutes, until it reduces and thickens slightly.

2. Add the langoustine tails and cook for 2 to 3 minutes, until warmed through. (If you are using fresh, uncooked langoustine, cook for another 2 minutes, until the shellfish are opaque but tender.) Add the basil, then add the cooked pasta, mixing thoroughly to coat with the sauce, and serve.

CREAMY LANGOUSTINE PASTA
WITH FRESH TOMATO SAUCE

A Family Affair

❧❧❧

AMY SCHERBER, BAKER, FOUNDER OF
AMY'S BREAD, AND AUTHOR OF TWO
COOKBOOKS, AND HER HUSBAND, TROY
ROHNE, SALES MANAGER OF AMY'S BREAD

Married: July 13, 2002

One of the sweetest perks of owning one of New York City's best bakeries—besides access to all those sweets—is the gratis dinners at restaurants bestowed by thankful chefs who serve the bread you bake. Amy Scherber is one such recipient, an award-winning baker and pastry chef, cookbook author, and owner of Amy's Bread—three bakeries that sell crusty loaves of rosemary rounds, black olive ficelle, and semolina-fennel bread to dozens of restaurants and thousands of devoted New Yorkers every day. She and her husband, Troy Rohne, the company sales manager, don't get much face time together at work, so they treasure the special occasions when they can break bread, so to speak, at posh city restaurants.

Back at their small apartment, their beloved 4-year-old son, Harry, demands much of their focus, so the couple seeks out creative ways to get him involved in the family dining experience. Amy had a revelation when she brought some dough home from the bakery and found that the most wonderful thing for a child is to squish his fingers through the warm mush. "And that's how we decided to make pizza," she says.

Cooking with a 4-year-old isn't as daunting as people might think, Amy notes. She prepares the dough, using a bit of extra yeast so it rises faster. The family then takes a play break and returns to the kitchen to stretch the now-puffy dough—which Harry loves—into three pizzas. The parents help their son dress his round with organic chunky tomato sauce, fresh herbs and mushrooms, olives, and lots of Parmesan. Harry puts his pizza on the stone first, and they bake, present, and eat each person's pizza one by one.

"This is the perfect fun family activity because the baking time is fairly quick and you can mess up the ingredients and still succeed in making a delicious meal," Amy says.

The master baker says that pizza is a great introduction for anyone new to baking and kneading because the crust is so forgiving. "If it's slightly soggy or too crusty, too loose or too stiff, it will still taste great. It's not like a loaf of bread that needs to be a certain shape."

ADVICE FOR NEWLYWEDS: *"I make notes about the recipe on a piece of paper and keep that paper tucked in the cookbook with the recipe. That way I can update ingredients and make the recipe better, just by trusting my intuition."*

—Amy

FAVORITE THING IN THE KITCHEN: *"A good pair of tongs. Between pulling stuff out of boiling water or bread from the toaster I can't live without them."*

—Amy

TAIWANESE BEEF NOODLE SOUP

Serves 2, with leftovers

In Taiwan, beef noodle soup is a vital part of the food culture, much like the hamburger is in America. Taiwanese foodies seek out the best bowl in town, in the same way Americans enjoy searching for the best burger in their city. Once you both try this savory broth, flavored with star anise, five-spice powder, and the addictive, slightly numbing heat of Szechuan peppercorns, you'll know why this dish has become an obsession for the Chinese. Use four red chilies if you like your soup spicy!

3 whole star anise, or ½ teaspoon ground star anise

1½ teaspoons whole Szechuan peppercorns*

2 to 4 small fresh red chilies, seeded (such as Thai bird chilies)

2 tablespoons vegetable or peanut oil

3 pounds bone-in beef shank or short rib, cut into four equal pieces

8 cloves garlic, lightly smashed with the heel of your knife

5 slices peeled fresh ginger, cut ¼ inch thick

5 green onions, cut into 4-inch pieces

¾ teaspoon Chinese five-spice powder*

3 tablespoons Chinese chili black bean sauce*

¼ cup Chinese rice wine (*shao hsing* wine or dry sherry)*

1 small piece Chinese rock sugar* or substitute 2 tablespoons dark brown sugar

⅓ cup light soy sauce

2 tablespoons dark soy sauce

6 cups low-sodium beef broth (preferably homemade)

2 cups water

1 bunch or more baby bok choy

¾ pound Asian noodles*, cooked and drained

2 tablespoons chopped fresh cilantro, for garnish

Chinese chili oil, for garnish (optional)*

*   *Available at Asian markets and specialty foods shops.*

1. In a cheesecloth, combine the star anise, peppercorns, and red chilies, and tie the bundle with a piece of kitchen string.

2. In a large heavy-bottomed pot or Dutch oven, heat the oil over high heat until it is smoking. Brown the beef on both sides, 2 to 3 minutes per side. Add the garlic, ginger, and green onions to the oil and stir until fragrant, about 2 minutes. Add the five-spice powder, chili black bean sauce, rice wine, rock sugar, light and dark soy sauces, broth, and water, as well as the spices bundled in the cheesecloth. Bring to a boil, then lower the heat to medium-low and cover. Simmer for $3\frac{1}{2}$ to 4 hours, until the meat is very tender and falling off the bone.

3. Remove the meat from the pot and discard the bones. Cut the meat into bite-size pieces. Strain the broth and discard the cheesecloth bundle, ginger, green onions, and garlic.

4. Cook the bok choy directly in the hot broth for 3 to 4 minutes, until tender. To serve, put a portion of the cooked noodles in each bowl and ladle the soup over the noodles. Add some of the beef and bok choy to the bowl, and garnish with a bit of cilantro and a dash of hot chili oil, if desired.

SLOW-COOKED LAMB RAGÙ

Serves 2

This hearty ragù is scrumptious whether you usually enjoy lamb or not. The richness of the sauce makes it the ideal comfort food as the days stretch from autumn into winter. The addition of pancetta and an aromatic blend of herbs make this ragù extra special—and a drizzle of half-and-half at the end rounds out the acidity in the tomato sauce. When the temperature dips this is one of the first recipes I turn to, much to my husband's delight. You may find you do the same!

2 tablespoons extra-virgin olive oil, divided

¼ pound pancetta or bacon, cut into ¼-inch pieces

1 medium sweet yellow onion, finely diced

2 ribs celery, finely diced

2 small carrots, finely diced

4 cloves garlic, finely minced

¾ cup dry white wine

1 pound ground lamb

½ teaspoon kosher salt

¼ teaspoon freshly ground black pepper

Small pinch of red pepper flakes (optional)

One 28-ounce can crushed tomatoes

2 tablespoons tomato paste

1 bay leaf

1 teaspoon chopped fresh thyme

1 teaspoon dried marjoram, or ½ teaspoon fresh chopped marjoram

½ teaspoon chopped fresh rosemary leaves

⅓ cup grated pecorino or Parmesan

¼ cup half-and-half or whole milk

½ pound pasta, cooked and drained

1. Heat a tablespoon of the olive oil in a large skillet over medium-high heat. Add the pancetta and cook until crisp, about 3 minutes. Remove the pancetta with a slotted spoon, leaving the drippings in the skillet, and transfer to a large, heavy-bottomed pot.

2. Add the onions to the pancetta drippings in the skillet, and cook until golden brown, about 7 to 8 minutes. Add the celery, carrots, and garlic, and cook for 5 minutes, or until the vegetables are soft. Add the wine, carefully scraping up the brown bits on the bottom of the skillet, and let it reduce for 2 minutes. Transfer the vegetables and wine to the pot with the pancetta.

3. Heat the remaining olive oil in the skillet, and brown the lamb over medium-high heat, 3 to 4 minutes. Add the salt, pepper, and red pepper flakes. Transfer the lamb to the pot.

4. Add the crushed tomatoes, tomato paste, bay leaf, thyme, marjoram, and rosemary to the pot. Simmer the sauce, uncovered, over medium-low heat for 2½ hours, stirring every 15 minutes or so. (If you see some orange-colored fat floating to the surface, scoop it up with a spoon and discard.)

5. Remove the bay leaf. Stir in the pecorino and half-and-half, and toss the ragù with the pasta.

Seasonal Feasts

KIMBERLY AND VITALY PALEY, CO-OWNERS
OF PALEY'S PLACE, PORTLAND, OREGON

Married: December 27, 1988

Kimberly and Vitaly Paley don't have children, but every spring they cook "potential Mother's and Father's Day dinners" for each other.

"We like to create a lot of special times together," Kimberly says. "When we have time off, we feast."

The couple owns Paley's Place, a Portland, Oregon, restaurant that served seasonal, organic, sustainable meals long before the rest of the world caught on. The Paleys bring that same appreciation for simple ingredients into their home.

"We don't eat out often," explains Vitaly, the executive chef, "because we'd rather spend our day off together at home."

So every Sunday morning they hop on their bicycles for a ride around nearby Sauvie Island, a small piece of rural land studded with farms and wildlife preserves. "I'm the cyclist guy, and she's the basket-on-her-bike kind of rider," Vitaly says. "We stop at the roadside stands and pick up whatever is in season, go home, and fire up the grill."

On a recent weekend, Vitaly took on the challenge of making a meal entirely on the grill using ingredients bought from island markets and culled from their backyard garden: goat cheese wrapped in chestnut leaves on charred flatbread; fava bean and mint purée; grilled Walla Walla onions, portobello mushrooms, sweet peppers, and new potatoes; cedar-plank salmon rubbed with brown sugar and lemon zest; and new strawberries and crème fraîche atop freshly baked lemon pound cake.

"Every time we sit down to a meal together, we say, 'Why would we go any place else?'" Vitaly laughs. "The simplest ingredients make the best-tasting meals."

As evidence, he recounts a surprise snowstorm that kept the couple confined to the house for days. Remembering when they lived in a one-bedroom apartment in New York and kept a hibachi in the fireplace, Vitaly put a whole chicken in a cast-iron skillet and cooked it right in the blazing fire. "We ate some of the chicken on the first night. The next day it became soup, the day after that it was salad, and on the last day it was chicken tacos. We ate so well thanks to that storm!"

Kimberly concurs, adding that the sweetest thing a couple can do is to cook without expectations. "Have no fear and follow no rules. Don't even think about what's proper or what's right or what's wrong. Whether your food is great or not is unimportant. What *is* important is creating memories."

ADVICE FOR NEWLYWEDS: *"Have no qualms about setting a beautiful table with flowers, old silver, and china. You might be having scrambled eggs, but man, scrambled eggs on Limoges is incredible!"* Also, *"Inspire your spouse with kitchen gifts, like specialty oils or skewers stuffed in the Christmas stockings."*

—*Kimberly*

FAVORITE THING IN THE KITCHEN: *"Le Creuset pots are an inspiration."*

—*Vitaly*

RED WINE AND MUSHROOM RISOTTO

Serves 2

When the first wild mushrooms of the season start popping up, grab your honey and beeline it to the farmers market, where you can buy a big bag of them for this risotto. Sautéing the mushrooms with a dribble of savory tamari (or dark soy sauce) helps bring out their meatiness—a little secret that will have you reaching for seconds.

3½ cups chicken stock

1½ cups dry red wine

1 tablespoon extra-virgin olive oil

4 tablespoons (½ stick) unsalted butter, divided

⅓ cup (about 1 large) finely diced shallots

½ pound fresh wild mushrooms (preferably porcini)

1½ teaspoons chopped fresh thyme

1 tablespoon chopped fresh parsley

1½ teaspoons tamari, or 1 teaspoon dark soy sauce

Kosher salt and freshly ground black pepper

⅔ cup (about 1 large) finely sliced leek, white parts only

1 cup arborio rice

⅔ cup grated Parmigiano-Reggiano

1 tablespoon snipped fresh chives

1½ teaspoons white truffle oil (optional)

1. Combine the chicken stock and wine in a stockpot and bring to a boil over medium heat. Lower the heat to a simmer and keep the liquids warm.

2. In a medium skillet, combine the olive oil, two tablespoons of the butter, and the shallots. Sauté the shallots over medium-high heat until they just begin to caramelize, about 3 to 4 minutes. Add the mushrooms, thyme, and parsley, and cook for 5 minutes, until the mushrooms are soft and any liquid evaporates. Add the tamari and toss to coat the mushrooms. Season lightly with salt and pepper. Remove the skillet from the heat and set aside.

3. Melt the remaining butter in a large saucepan over medium heat. Add the leeks and sauté for 2 minutes. Add the arborio rice and stir for 2 minutes, until the grains are toasted and well coated with the butter and leeks. Stir in a ladle of the warm stock-wine mixture and cook until the rice has absorbed it all. On medium heat, add the remaining stock one ladle at a time, letting the rice absorb the liquid completely before adding more. The risotto should have fully absorbed the liquid after about 30 minutes (taste the rice to make sure it has cooked through and add more salt and pepper to taste).

4. If the stock evaporates too quickly and the rice is not yet cooked, add $1/3$ cup of water to the pan and stir. The water will evaporate and help the rice cook, without changing the flavor of the risotto. Stir the mushroom-shallot mixture and Parmigiano-Reggiano into the rice. Spoon the risotto into serving bowls and top each bowl with a sprinkle of chives and a drizzle of white truffle oil, if desired.

MENU

A Soul–Satisfying Menu for a Cozy Night In

My Award-Winning Four-Cheese Mac-and-Cheese, page 79

Fall-Apart Pot Roast, page 153

Samoa Blondies, page 183

Losing the Newlywed 15
HEALTHFUL VEGETABLE
SIDE DISHES

Parmesan-Roasted Asparagus, Tomatoes, and Eggs

Smoky-Sweet Corn Pudding

Roasted Parmesan Broccoli with Toasted Bread Crumbs

Warm Roasted Potatoes with Basil Pesto

Romesco Sauce

Pasta Salad with Arugula and Cherry Tomatoes

Creamy Dijon Potato Salad

Maple-Roasted Root Vegetables with Sherry Vinegar

Light Eggplant and Basil Pasta

"HARMONY ONLY OCCURS FROM OVERCOMING CHALLENGES.
TAKE ON CHALLENGING MEALS. IF YOU CAN GET
BEYOND THE TENSION THE CHALLENGE CREATES,
YOU'LL HAVE HARMONY, AND THAT IS REWARDING."

—James E. McWilliams, *author of* Just Food

PARMESAN-ROASTED ASPARAGUS, TOMATOES, AND EGGS

Serves 2

This dish is especially good in the early summer, when local asparagus and tomatoes start appearing at the farmers markets. The grape tomatoes are roasted alongside the asparagus in this recipe, until their delicate skins just begin to pucker and their juices run warm and sweet. Top each portion with an egg fried in olive oil, and puncture the soft orange yolks so they dribble all over the asparagus, like the richest sauce imaginable.

> 1 pound asparagus
> 1 cup grape or cherry tomatoes
> 3 tablespoons extra-virgin olive oil, divided
> 1/4 cup grated Parmesan or pecorino
> 1/2 teaspoon kosher salt
> 1/2 teaspoon freshly ground black pepper
> 2 large eggs
> 3 spoonfuls Basil Pesto (page 107, optional but delicious!)

1. Preheat the oven to 425°F.

2. Wash the asparagus. Break the bottom stems off and discard. Toss the asparagus spears and tomatoes in 2 tablespoons of the olive oil, then place them on a parchment- or Silpat-lined baking sheet. Sprinkle the Parmesan, salt, and pepper over the vegetables. Roast the vegetables for 12 to 14 minutes, or until tender and cooked through.

3. Meanwhile, fry the two eggs in the remaining olive oil, seasoning them with salt and pepper to taste. Place an egg on each portion of the cooked vegetables, and top with a dab of Basil Pesto.

Healthful Vegetable Side Dishes

SMOKY-SWEET CORN PUDDING

Serves 2

Sweet corn is one of the best parts of summer. But since the season for truly tender, local corn is fleeting, this recipe was born from a desire to capture its wonderful taste year-round. The plump kernels are cooked with soft leeks and bacon, then baked with butter and some light cream to make an irresistible corn pudding. This is especially good with Grilled Porterhouse Steak with Blue Cheese Butter (page 135).

1 tablespoon vegetable oil

4 strips bacon, cut into $^1/_4$-inch pieces

$^1/_2$ cup (about 1 medium) finely sliced leek, white and light green parts only

1 large egg

$^1/_2$ cup half-and-half

1 tablespoon unsalted butter, melted

3 teaspoons flour

$^1/_3$ teaspoon kosher salt

Pinch of freshly ground black pepper

$1^1/_4$ cup corn kernels (fresh or frozen)

$^1/_2$ teaspoon sweet paprika

1. Preheat the oven to 350°F.

2. Heat the vegetable oil in a medium skillet over medium-high heat. Add the bacon and cook until crisp, about 3 minutes. Add the leeks and sauté until they soften and begin to brown, about 2 minutes. With a slotted spoon, remove the bacon and the leeks and set aside.

3. In a medium bowl, whisk together the egg and half-and-half. Stir in the butter, flour, salt, pepper, corn, and paprika. Add the cooked bacon and leeks. (If you are feeling decadent, add 1 tablespoon of the bacon drippings into the mixture as well.)

4. Ladle the mixture into two individual ramekins and bake for 30 to 35 minutes, or until the puddings slightly puff. Let cool for several minutes, then serve.

ROASTED PARMESAN BROCCOLI WITH TOASTED BREAD CRUMBS

Serves 2

A lot of people don't particularly care for vegetables, unless they're done really well. But this recipe is something you can both enjoy cooking because it's easy and tasty. Roasting the broccoli in the oven gives it a deliciously nutty flavor, and a dusting of seasoned panko (extra-crunchy Japanese bread crumbs) wakes up your palate with an irresistible crunch.

> 1 head broccoli, cut into florets
> 3 tablespoons extra-virgin olive oil
> 1 teaspoon kosher salt
> ¼ teaspoon freshly ground black pepper
> 3 cloves garlic, minced
> ¼ teaspoon red pepper flakes (optional)
> 3 tablespoons grated Parmesan
> 1 tablespoon unsalted butter
> ⅓ cup panko (or substitute regular bread crumbs)

1. Preheat the oven to 400°F.

2. Place the broccoli florets on a parchment- or Silpat-lined baking sheet and drizzle with the olive oil. Sprinkle the salt, pepper, garlic, red pepper flakes, and Parmesan evenly over the broccoli.

3. Roast the broccoli for 20 minutes, or until it is cooked through and the florets have just started to turn brown. Meanwhile, in a small skillet over medium heat, melt the butter and toast the panko until it is golden brown and crisp. Sprinkle the toasted panko over the broccoli before serving.

The Good Life

❧

DUSKIE ESTES AND JOHN STEWART, CHEF-
OWNERS AND PROPRIETORS OF ZAZU RESTAURANT
+ FARM, BOVOLO RESTAURANT, AND BLACK PIG
MEAT CO. IN SONOMA COUNTY, CALIFORNIA

Married: March 25, 2000

It's hard to imagine how this chef-owner couple can find time to eat together. With children to care for, two restaurants, and a three-acre farm, quality time at the table seems ridiculous.

But Duskie Estes and John Stewart are believers in sitting down at the table, so carving out family time is an essential way of life. For them, that means involving their daughters MacKenzie and Brydie in the process of cooking for the family, rather than finding ways to distract them so they can take on the cooking themselves.

"Kids are process oriented," John says. "Peeling the carrot becomes the thing, not making the soup."

The couple built an outdoor kitchen on their sunny farm, complete with a huge wood-fired pizza oven among the chickens, pigs, sheep, fruit trees, and vegetable gardens. Days off are spent as a family in the backyard.

On a typical day at home, John takes their daughters to the pizza oven where they help gather wood and watch him light the fire. They'll make the dough—John puts the yeast and water together while the girls measure the flour—pick and prepare pizza toppings (such as fresh basil, tomatoes, and asparagus), and gather a salad while the dough rises. The girls might also grate cheese and collect eggs from the chicken coop, or help harvest the garden or olives, lemons, and peaches from the trees. Later, John might make a big batch of fresh fruit jelly while the girls shape the dough into balls and roll out the pizzas. For dessert they eat homemade gelato, made of ingredients such as seasonal bing cherries with chocolate chips.

"It's the opposite of how we cook in the restaurant," John says. "We'll spend the whole day on long, drawn-out projects like braiding onions or feeding the fire."

"Cooking is the art of giving," Duskie adds. "It's as basic as making the coffee if you are the first one up in the morning. Making nourishment is a gift from the heart, and we want our kids to experience giving too."

ADVICE FOR NEWLYWEDS: *"Don't be afraid to burn things. We burn things every day. You can learn a great deal from failure."*

—John

"There are so many things to love about a person other than how they cut a carrot. What is really important is not the shape of the carrot. The point is that you love each other, and you're having fun together."

—Duskie

FAVORITE THINGS IN THE KITCHEN: *"Wood-fired pizza oven and Italian gelato machine."*

—Duskie and John

WARM ROASTED POTATOES WITH BASIL PESTO

Serves 2, with leftovers

Tossing golden-brown, crisp-roasted potatoes in this delicious fresh pesto is a new take on the traditional potato side dish, and it is absolutely wonderful whether hot or cold. Try the leftover pesto in a cold pasta salad or in a tomato mozzarella panini. This versatile recipe is one you'll use again and again.

1½ pounds Yukon Gold or fingerling potatoes, cut into bite-size pieces
4 tablespoons extra-virgin olive oil
¾ teaspoon kosher salt
Pinch or two of red pepper flakes
Basil Pesto (recipe follows)

1. Preheat the oven to 400°F.

2. Place the potatoes on a parchment- or Silpat-lined baking sheet and drizzle with the olive oil. Add the salt and red pepper and toss to coat. Bake the potatoes for 20 minutes, then flip them over with a spatula. Bake them for another 20 minutes, or until the potatoes are golden brown.

3. Transfer the potatoes to a large bowl and add ½ cup of pesto. Toss to coat, then add a little more pesto if you'd like.

BASIL PESTO

Makes about 1 cup of pesto

> **2 cups packed fresh basil**
> **$^2/_3$ cup extra-virgin olive oil (plus up to 2 additional tablespoons)**
> **$^1/_3$ cup toasted pine nuts**
> **3 cloves garlic, minced**
> **$^1/_2$ cup grated Parmesan**
> **$^1/_4$ teaspoon kosher salt**
> **$^1/_8$ teaspoon freshly ground black pepper**

1. Combine all ingredients in a food processor and process until smooth. If the resulting pesto is too thick for your liking, add the extra tablespoons olive oil and process again to combine. (Leftover pesto can be covered and stored in the refrigerator for up to 3 days.)

ROMESCO SAUCE

Makes 2¼ cups of sauce

During grilling season, there is absolutely no vegetable dish more delicious than charred leeks smothered in this bracing romesco. This sauce is a lovely thing to make when one of you starts complaining about those jeans feeling a little snug—chock-full of vegetables, nuts, and olive oil, it's quite possibly one of the healthiest things you two can eat! The sauce keeps for up to five days, so try the leftovers on grilled shrimp, pork, pasta, or simply on some bread for a light and delicious snack.

> **2 medium tomatoes, quartered**
> **3 tablespoons sherry vinegar (plus 1 additional teaspoon if you like a little more acidity)**
> **¼ cup extra-virgin olive oil**
> **⅓ cup cubed stale bread (a baguette is best)**
> **1 roasted red bell pepper**
> **4 cloves garlic, finely diced**
> **8 almonds, toasted and chopped**
> **¼ cup hazelnuts, toasted, skins removed, and chopped**
> **½ teaspoon kosher salt**
> **Small pinch of red pepper flakes**
> **1 teaspoon sweet or smoked paprika**

1. Preheat the oven to 400°F.

2. Place the tomatoes on a parchment- or Silpat-lined baking sheet and roast for 15 minutes, or until softened.

3. In a large bowl, combine the vinegar and olive oil. Add the bread and soak until softened, about 5 minutes.

4. Combine the bread (and vinegar and oil used to soak the bread), roasted tomatoes, red bell pepper, garlic, almonds, hazelnuts, salt, red pepper flakes, and paprika in a food processor and process until smooth.

ROMESCO SAUCE

Chariots of Fillet

❧

LEILA KEMPNER AND HER HUSBAND, JAMES
E. MCWILLIAMS, AUTHOR OF *JUST FOOD*

Married: March 18, 1995

When Leila Kempner and James McWilliams were first dating while in college in Washington, D.C., cooking together was one of the ways they bonded as a couple.

"Very early on there was an interest in trying new recipes and challenging ourselves with new foods," James says. "Over time simple meals became elaborate meals."

Living frugally, the couple made their own urban adventures by seeking out unusual ingredients in D.C.'s farmers markets and ethnic shops and restaurants, and also by mastering traditional dishes, such as ratatouille and homemade pasta.

At one point the couple became "addicted" to the Maryland rockfish sold across town by their favorite fishmonger. James, a long-distance runner, was so dedicated to obtaining a fish to grill for their evening meal that he planned his course around the fishmonger's schedule and ran several miles through the streets of D.C. with a whole 3-pound rockfish in his backpack.

"I can't imagine what people were thinking," James remembers. "But we were so into these cooking projects of ours that it didn't seem like a big deal to go running while carrying that night's meal on my back."

Later, when James became a vegetarian, Leila, though not a vegetarian, dedicated herself to exploring the spices and flavors of Indian and Southeast Asian cooking with her husband, so they could continue to draw big flavors from their meals together.

Now the couple has two children, and, while their daily habits have changed, they say cooking is a part of who they are, and they have made a commitment to not abandon it.

"The sacrifice is that we sometimes eat at 10:30 at night," James says, "which is not great for your health, but it's great for your relationship. Families that eat together become closer. It's inevitable."

ADVICE FOR NEWLYWEDS: *"Allow yourself to overindulge one or two days a week and enjoy yourself. 'Everything in moderation' is a good philosophy, but every now and then you should have a little more wine."*

—James

FAVORITE THING IN THE KITCHEN: *"Kitchen tongs. I love them: you can toss a salad, pick up food, or pluck things out of boiling water."*

—James

PASTA SALAD WITH ARUGULA
AND CHERRY TOMATOES

Serves 2

This recipe is a way to show off the best produce you can find, so seek out the juiciest local tomatoes, the sweetest basil, the brightest mint, and the freshest, most peppery arugula. Once you stir the Greek feta into the pasta, it mellows out the acidity in this simple lemon and olive oil vinaigrette for a light sauce that coats each tender grain of orzo. This salad is fantastic with any grilled meat, such as Sweet-and-Hot Chicken Kebabs (page 126).

FOR THE PASTA:

1 medium tomato, preferably heirloom, cut into bite-size pieces,
   or ³/₄ cup cherry tomatoes, halved

¹/₄ cup chopped fresh basil

1 tablespoon chopped fresh mint

²/₃ cup (about ¹/₂ large) finely diced red bell pepper

¹/₄ cup (about 1 medium) finely minced shallots

³/₄ cup orzo, cooked and drained

³/₄ cup packed arugula or baby spinach, torn into bite-size pieces

¹/₄ cup toasted pine nuts

2¹/₂ ounces (about ¹/₂ cup) Greek feta, diced

FOR THE DRESSING:

2 tablespoons freshly squeezed lemon juice (plus up to 1 additional
   tablespoon)

3 tablespoons extra-virgin olive oil

¹/₂ teaspoon paprika

Kosher salt and freshly ground black pepper

1. To make the pasta, in a large bowl combine the tomatoes, basil, mint, red bell pepper, shallots, and cooked orzo.

2. In a separate bowl, whisk together the ingredients for the dressing.

3. Pour the dressing over the pasta and vegetables and stir to combine. Just before serving, add the arugula, pine nuts, and feta. Toss again to combine and check for seasoning, adding 1 tablespoon lemon juice if desired. Serve at room temperature.

CREAMY DIJON POTATO SALAD

Serves 2 generously

Many people don't care for overly gloopy, mayonnaise-heavy potato salads, so the dressing for this salad is thinned with an equal amount of Dijon mustard. Not only does the mustard lend a lot of flavor, but it also cuts the fat in half, for a lighter salad everyone will enjoy. Make a few extra servings for your next backyard barbecue or pack it up for a two-person picnic.

> **1 pound Yukon Gold or fingerling potatoes, cut into bite-size pieces**
> **¼ cup mayonnaise (you can use low-fat)**
> **1 tablespoon freshly squeezed lemon juice**
> **¼ cup Dijon mustard**
> **1 teaspoon dried mustard**
> **⅓ cup diced red onion**
> **3 tablespoons chopped fresh parsley**
> **4 large hard-boiled eggs, diced**
> **⅓ cup cooked bacon crumbles or chopped ham (optional)**
> **Kosher salt and freshly ground black pepper**

1. Cook the potatoes in boiling, salted water for 25 minutes, or until tender. Drain and let cool.

2. In a large bowl, whisk together the mayonnaise, lemon juice, Dijon mustard, and dried mustard. Stir in the onion and parsley. Add the cooked potatoes to the dressing, and toss until combined. Taste, and add more lemon juice if you'd like. Gently fold in the eggs and bacon, and season with salt and pepper.

Healthful Vegetable Side Dishes

Garden of Plenty

JOSH LOEB AND ZOE NATHAN, CO-OWNERS
OF RUSTIC CANYON WINE BAR & SEASONAL
KITCHEN AND HUCKLEBERRY BAKERY AND
CAFÉ IN SANTA MONICA, CALIFORNIA

Married: January 11, 2009

Josh Loeb and Zoe Nathan met at Rustic Canyon, Josh's wine bar and restaurant, where Zoe was working as the house pastry chef. They quickly began dating, fell in love, and discovered that even beyond their jobs, food was an important part of their life together.

"Our first road trip together was up to Portland, Oregon, and the Willamette Valley to eat at all of the great restaurants, bakeries, and coffee shops we had been reading about," Josh recalls. "A snowstorm closed the roads and kept us stuck in the city, and we spent days on a culinary tour, walking from place to place and bonding over food."

When the couple married, they eschewed the traditional wedding registries and instead registered for something they knew they'd really use: a culinary garden. Guests contributed money toward a full overhaul of the couple's driveway: the concrete was ripped out, and a garden landscaping operation came in and built and planted a raised-bed organic garden, complete with a little seating area for the newlyweds to share a pot of tea or bottle of wine while eating the meals they'd created from their bounty. After the first batch of crops came up, they harvested in a single week a Southern California mother lode, including blueberries and strawberries, Maui onions, tomatoes, eggplants, baby lettuces, and assorted greens. Josh and Zoe found they couldn't wait to get home and see what new produce was sprouting forth in their private oasis. Cooking had always been a pleasure, and it took on a new level of excitement as they created fresh-from-the-garden sauces and salsas and the best caponata they'd ever tasted.

"Having this space and a place to channel our energies really grounds us from the chaos of the restaurant and bakery," Josh says. "It's our little safe haven to hide out in on our day off. All we want to do is cook together and enjoy each other."

ADVICE FOR NEWLYWEDS: *"Find ways to make your dining experiences intimate and special to you. We like informality, so sometimes we eat dinner sitting on the floor at the coffee table or at the bar at restaurants instead of in the dining room."*

—*Josh*

FAVORITE THINGS IN THE KITCHEN: *"Besides our new garden, having a hand-immersion blender for making soup, a really good ceramic knife, and a nice set of pots and pans makes cooking so much more enjoyable."*

—*Josh*

MAPLE-ROASTED ROOT
VEGETABLES WITH
SHERRY VINEGAR

MAPLE-ROASTED ROOT VEGETABLES WITH SHERRY VINEGAR

Serves 8 to 10

When the temperature drops and the holiday season rolls around, root vegetables caramelized and covered in the autumnal flavor of maple syrup are just the thing to serve to a crowd. The vegetables in this recipe are roasted with rosemary until their natural sugars brown, then tossed in a piquant sweet-and-tangy dressing while they're still hot. This recipe feeds a holiday crowd, but also reheats well when leftovers are portioned out for two.

1¼ pound sweet potatoes peeled and sliced into 1-inch-thick wedges
1 pound parsnips, peeled and sliced into ½-inch-thick pieces
1 pound carrots, peeled and sliced into ½-inch-thick pieces
2 teaspoons chopped fresh thyme
1 tablespoon chopped fresh rosemary leaves
2 teaspoons kosher salt
1 teaspoon freshly ground black pepper
¼ cup extra-virgin olive oil
¼ cup pure maple syrup, preferably Grade B
2 tablespoons sherry vinegar
2 tablespoons chicken stock

1. Preheat the oven to 400°F.

2. Divide the sweet potatoes, parsnips, and carrots in two roasting pans. Sprinkle the vegetables with the thyme, rosemary, salt, pepper, and olive oil, tossing to coat.

3. Roast the vegetables for about 45 to 50 minutes, until they are lightly browned and tender when pierced with a fork.

4. In a large bowl, whisk together the maple syrup, sherry vinegar, and chicken stock. Add the roasted vegetables and toss them with the liquid to coat. Transfer the vegetables to a platter and serve.

LIGHT EGGPLANT AND BASIL PASTA

Serves 2

Sometimes you have to balance out all that fried chicken and pie with something a little lighter. This easy-to-prepare, vegetarian eggplant pasta is a tasty way for you both to get back on track.

> 2 tablespoons extra-virgin olive oil
> $^1/_2$ medium sweet yellow onion, finely diced
> 2 cloves garlic, finely diced
> 1 small Italian eggplant, cut into $^1/_4$-inch cubes
> $^3/_4$ teaspoon kosher salt
> $^1/_2$ teaspoon freshly ground black pepper
> Small pinch red pepper flakes (optional)
> $1^1/_2$ cups tomato sauce
> $^1/_3$ cup dry white wine
> $^1/_4$ cup diced pitted black olives
> $^1/_2$ cup torn fresh basil leaves, divided
> 3 ounces fresh mozzarella, diced
> 8 ounces whole wheat spaghetti, cooked

1. Heat the olive oil in a medium skillet over medium-high heat. Add the onions and garlic and sauté until lightly golden brown, about 5 to 6 minutes. Add the eggplant, salt, pepper, and red pepper flakes. Cook for 3 to 4 minutes, or until the eggplant softens, then add the tomato sauce, wine, olives, and half the basil leaves. Lower the heat to medium and simmer the sauce for 5 minutes, then turn off the heat. Add the mozzarella (the residual heat from the sauce will melt it slightly).

2. Toss the spaghetti with the eggplant sauce and top with the remaining basil.

MENU

A Holiday with the Family

Blue Cheese Crackers, page 18

Holiday Rib Roast with Thyme Gravy, page 139

Creamy Kale Gratin, page 84

Maple-Roasted Root Vegetables with Sherry Vinegar, page 117

Pumpkin Brioche Bread Pudding with Warm Maple Cream, page 196

Something Bold, Something New
MEAT, POULTRY & SEAFOOD DISHES

Steamed Clams in White Wine with Chorizo

Mediterranean-Style Tuna

Sweet-and-Hot Chicken Kebabs

Coconut Curried Crab

Chicken Piccata with Mushrooms and Leeks

The Ultimate Roast Chicken

Grilled Porterhouse Steak with Blue Cheese Butter

Balsamic-Glazed Turkey Meat Loaf

Holiday Rib Roast with Thyme Gravy

Cornmeal-Crusted Fried Fish Fillets with Homemade Tartar Sauce

Pancetta-Wrapped Pork with Gorgonzola Sauce

Cheddar Cheese Grits with Shrimp and Bacon Gravy

Extra-Cheesy Classic Lasagna

Fall Apart Pot Roast

Ultra-Crispy Secret Fried Chicken

Rack of Lamb with Sour Cherries, Cauliflower, and Capers

Italian Grandmother Meatballs

Super Bowl Chili

Backyard Barbecue Mile-High Burgers and Buttermilk Onion Rings

Paprika-Spiced Hungarian Beef Goulash

Chicken Potpies with Cheddar-Thyme Crusts

Bourbon-Glazed Baby Back Ribs with Sweet-and-Smoky Barbecue Sauce

Braised Short Ribs with Salsa Verde and Horseradish Cream

"GET OUT OF THE HOUSE MORE OFTEN. GROW SOMETHING.
CATCH A FISH. GENERATE A BIT OF EXCITEMENT
AND FIND WAYS TO MAKE COOKING MORE FUN THAN
HEATING SOMETHING UP FROM THE STORE."

—Steven Rinella, *author of* American Buffalo *and* The Scavenger's Guide to Haute Cuisine

STEAMED CLAMS IN WHITE WINE WITH CHORIZO

Serves 2

Clams and chorizo are a classic combination—there's something about the slightly spicy, meaty flavor of the sausage that makes the sweet, briny taste of steamed clams even more seductive. Need I tell you the broth is amazing? Be sure to have plenty of crusty bread on hand for dipping.

> 1 tablespoon extra-virgin olive oil
> 3 tablespoons unsalted butter
> ½ cup finely chopped sweet yellow onion
> ¼ pound dried chorizo links, thinly sliced
> 1 small tomato, coarsely chopped
> 2 cloves garlic, finely minced
> 2 pounds littleneck clams, scrubbed
> ½ cup dry white wine
> ¼ cup chicken stock
> Small pinch of red pepper flakes
> Kosher salt
> 2 lemon wedges, for garnish
> Fresh parsley, chopped, for sprinkling

1. In a large, heavy-bottomed pan or Dutch oven with a lid, combine the olive oil and butter over medium-high heat. Add the onions and cook until they start to soften, about 3 minutes. Add the chorizo and let it brown for about 2 to 3 minutes. Add the tomato, garlic, clams, wine, chicken stock, and red pepper flakes, and cover to allow the clams to steam. After about 3 to 5 minutes, all the clams should have opened (discard any that have refused to open after 5 minutes). Season the broth with salt to taste.

2. Pour the clams and the broth into two big bowls and garnish with a squeeze of lemon and a sprinkling of parsley. Dip thick slices of your favorite bread in the broth.

Meat, Poultry & Seafood Dishes

MEDITERRANEAN-STYLE TUNA

MEDITERRANEAN-STYLE TUNA

Serves 2

William Belickis is one of the best chefs in Seattle. For his 40th birthday, he rented out a room at a local Italian restaurant, where they served the most delicious prosciutto, tomato, olive, and anchovy snack bites before dinner. The next day, spurred by a craving for the same flavors, I created this quick and simple tuna recipe. You'll both love the combination of these Mediterranean ingredients—they add such dimension to a simple piece of cooked fish! Best of all, this dish comes together in about ten minutes.

> Two 6-ounce tuna fillets, about $^3/_4$ inch thick
> Kosher salt and freshly ground black pepper
> 3 tablespoons extra-virgin olive oil, divided
> 3 slices prosciutto, cut into $^1/_2$-inch pieces
> $^1/_4$ cup diced sun-dried tomatoes
> $^1/_2$ cup oil-marinated artichoke hearts, cut into bite-size pieces
> 8 kalamata olives, pitted and diced
> 1 roasted red bell pepper, chopped into bite-size pieces
> 4 anchovies, finely diced
> $^1/_2$ cup packed salad greens, such as arugula, watercress, or spinach
> Squeeze of fresh lemon juice

1. Season the tuna lightly with salt and pepper. Heat 1 tablespoon of the olive oil in a large skillet over medium-high heat. Add the tuna and sear to your desired doneness: about $1^1/_2$ minutes per side for rare, $2^1/_2$ minutes per side for medium.

2. In a large bowl, combine the prosciutto, sun-dried tomatoes, artichoke hearts, olives, red bell pepper, anchovies, and greens. Add the remaining olive oil and the lemon juice and toss to coat. Pile the mixture on top of the tuna and serve.

Meat, Poultry & Seafood Dishes

SWEET-AND-HOT CHICKEN KEBABS

Serves 2, with leftovers

Chicken breasts can sometimes be dry and flavorless, especially when served skinless and cooked off the bone. Not so with this recipe, where pieces of chicken are marinated in a lovely honey, wine, garlic, and lemon juice mixture. A bit of kick from the cayenne keeps things interesting and balances the sweet, tangy marinade.

> 3 tablespoons honey
> 3 tablespoons extra-virgin olive oil
> 2 tablespoons dry white wine
> $^3/_4$ teaspoon kosher salt
> 3 cloves garlic, minced
> $1^1/_2$ tablespoons freshly squeezed lemon juice
> $^1/_4$ teaspoon cayenne
> 2 tablespoons chopped fresh parsley
> 1 pound boneless white and/or dark chicken meat, cut into
>   2-inch cubes
> 15 cremini or button mushrooms
> 15 cherry tomatoes

1. In a large bowl, whisk together the honey, olive oil, wine, salt, garlic, lemon juice, cayenne, and parsley. Add the chicken to the marinade, mixing to coat. Let the chicken marinate for at least 1 hour, or preferably overnight. During the last half hour, add the mushrooms and tomatoes to the marinade so they absorb some of the flavor.

2. Preheat an indoor or outdoor grill to medium-high heat.

3. Thread the chicken, tomatoes, and mushrooms onto metal skewers. Grill for 8 to 10 minutes total, or until the chicken is cooked through. (Cut into a piece of the chicken to check if it is fully cooked.)

SWEET-AND-HOT
CHICKEN KEBABS

COCONUT CURRIED CRAB

Serves 2

The next time the craving for Indian take-out strikes, why not try this coconut curried crab instead? The creamy coconut milk and gentle spices perfume the sweet crab and render this easy, ten-minute dish unforgettable. I like to serve this with naan (Indian flat bread) or basmati rice.

$^1\!/_4$ **cup ghee or vegetable oil**

1 tablespoon brown mustard seeds (optional)

1 tablespoon finely diced peeled fresh ginger

2 to 6 (depending on your heat preference) small red chilies (such as Bird's Eye), finely diced

1 medium yellow onion, finely diced

2 teaspoons turmeric

3 teaspoons garam masala*

$^2\!/_3$ **cup full-fat coconut milk**

1 pound cooked crabmeat

2 teaspoons light brown sugar

1 teaspoon kosher salt

$^1\!/_4$ **teaspoon freshly ground black pepper**

Freshly squeezed lime juice

Chopped fresh cilantro (optional)

1. In a large sauté pan over medium-high heat, melt the ghee. Add the mustard seeds and roast until they pop and smell nutty, about 1 minute. Add the ginger, chilies, and onions and sauté for 6 to 7 minutes, or until the onions soften and turn golden brown.

2. Add the turmeric, garam masala, and coconut milk to the pan. Stir until the spices coat the onions, then add the crabmeat and brown sugar, and simmer for 2 to 3 minutes, or until heated through. Add the salt and pepper, and stir in lime juice to taste. Serve topped with a sprinkle of cilantro, if desired.

---

* *Ground garam masala is available at specialty food shops and some supermarkets.*

CHICKEN PICCATA WITH MUSHROOMS AND LEEKS

Serves 2

The secret to making a good chicken piccata is to let the sauce reduce so all that's left is an intensely flavored, richly dark, syrupy sauce that, combined with the bright citrus and capers, coats each morsel of chicken. The leeks and mushrooms lend some dimension (and nutrition) to this much-loved classic, which is sure to become a favorite quickie weeknight recipe for the two of you.

> **2 boneless, skinless chicken breasts (about 1 pound total), butterflied***
> **Kosher salt and freshly ground black pepper**
> **2 tablespoons grated Parmesan**
> **3 tablespoons flour**
> **3 tablespoons unsalted butter, divided**
> **2 tablespoons extra-virgin olive oil**
> **1 cup sliced cremini mushrooms**
> **³⁄₄ cup (about 1 large) sliced leek, white parts only**
> **2 teaspoons minced fresh garlic**
> **3 tablespoons freshly squeezed lemon juice**
> **¹⁄₃ cup chicken stock (preferably homemade)**
> **3 tablespoons dry white wine**
> **2 tablespoons capers, drained**
> **3 tablespoons chopped fresh parsley**

1. Place the chicken breasts between two sheets of plastic wrap and pound with a meat mallet (or a small cast-iron pan) until they are ¼ inch thick. Season the chicken very lightly with salt and pepper (not too much, since the capers in the sauce add salt). On a plate, combine the Parmesan and flour; dredge the chicken pieces in the cheese mixture and shake off the excess.

---

* *To butterfly a piece of meat, simply place one hand on top of the meat and slide the knife through the meat with the knife parallel to the cutting board, stopping before you cut all the way through. (You are essentially slicing the meat widthwise.) Open up the piece of meat, and you'll have a larger, thinner piece than the one you started with.*

Meat, Poultry & Seafood Dishes

129

CHICKEN PICCATA WITH
MUSHROOMS AND LEEKS

2. In a large skillet over medium-high heat, melt 2 tablespoons of the butter; add the olive oil. Cook the chicken breasts for 3 minutes per side, or until juices run clear when the tip of a knife is inserted into the center. Remove the chicken from the pan and keep warm.

3. Add the mushrooms and leeks to the skillet and sauté for 2 to 3 minutes, or until softened. Add the garlic, lemon juice, chicken stock, wine, capers, and parsley. Reduce the liquid in the pan by about two thirds, until the sauce is thickened and syrupy. Add the remaining butter to the sauce, and stir until combined. Spoon the sauce over the chicken and serve.

Humble Beginnings

JOHN AND SUKEY JAMISON, FOUNDERS OF
JAMISON FARM IN LATROBE, PENNSYLVANIA

Married: March 29, 1969

John and Sukey Jamison both had an early interest in food, but they could have never foretold what a starring role haute cuisine would eventually play in their lives. Working at Barack Obama's presidential inauguration alongside Alice Waters, swapping recipes with Daniel Boulud, advising Jean-Louis Palladin on how best to cook lamb shanks, and "communing" over a bottle of Châteauneuf-du-Pape with Julia Child were not even glimmers in their imaginations when the newlyweds were living in Kansas City in the early 1970s. This was before the Jamisons moved to Pennsylvania, purchased two hundred acres, and began raising the grass-fed sheep that some of the world's greatest chefs call America's best. It was one night in the '70s, and the young couple had invited their favorite college professor to their apartment for a simple but elegant dinner. They had the idea of creating a European-style meal of slow-cooked pot roast, fresh country bread, and sparkling conversation fueled by Sukey's old-world cooking and an exquisite bottle of Bordeaux supplied by their professor.

"I remember reading through the recipe and so many elements didn't look right," recalls Sukey, who was already an accomplished home cook at this point. "But I didn't trust my instincts; I trusted the recipe, and that was that."

The meat—which was no small sacrifice at the time—burned to a crisp and was completely inedible.

"So what did we do? We laughed and sat around and drank that great bottle of wine," John recalls. "We told stories all night and had a wonderful time! It just goes to show that you should never be afraid to try anything. If you've got a decent loaf of bread and a good bottle of wine, how bad can it be?"

Today Sukey and John still cook together almost every night—though their meat dishes are far more successful than that doomed pot roast back in Kansas City. They love cooking for friends in their rural community and introducing them to the classic, gourmet foods they've come to appreciate: Hudson Valley foie gras, organic vegetables plucked straight from the Jamisons' garden, and, of course, tender and succulent lamb.

"Food is the center of our life," John says. "We had no idea what we were doing in the beginning, but we threw ourselves into it and learned to trust our instincts, and that has brought wonderful people—and food—into our life."

ADVICE FOR NEWLYWEDS: *"Never worry about burning the pot roast."*

—John

FAVORITE THINGS IN THE KITCHEN: *"Fresh herbs and a KitchenAid stand mixer."*

—Sukey

THE ULTIMATE ROAST CHICKEN

Serves 6

To make the ultimate roast chicken, you'll have to start two days before you want to serve it. Most recipes just call for a sprinkle of salt, pepper, and herbs before the chicken goes into the oven, which results in salty chicken skin and bland meat. The chicken in this recipe is rubbed with the seasonings, then allowed to rest in the refrigerator for two days. This method allows the salt to penetrate the meat, and the chicken becomes very flavorful all the way to the bone, just as it should be.

> **One 5-pound roasting chicken**
> **1¹⁄₂ tablespoons kosher salt**
> **2 teaspoons freshly ground black pepper**
> **2 tablespoons chopped fresh thyme, rosemary, or marjoram**
> **4 cloves garlic, cut into ¹⁄₄-inch slices**
> **1 small onion, quartered**
> **2 bay leaves**
> **3 tablespoons extra-virgin olive oil**

1. Rub the chicken all over with the salt, pepper, chopped herbs, and garlic. Cover and refrigerate the chicken for 2 days to allow the flavors to penetrate.

2. Preheat the oven to 425°F.

3. Stuff the onion quarters and bay leaves into the chicken's cavity. Pour the olive oil over the surface of the chicken. Place the chicken in a roasting pan fitted with a roasting rack.

4. Roast the chicken for 25 minutes at 425°F, then turn down the temperature to 375°F. Roast the chicken for approximately 1 hour more, or until the juices run clear and a meat thermometer inserted in the thigh registers 165°F. Let the chicken rest for at least 10 minutes before carving.

GRILLED PORTERHOUSE STEAK
WITH BLUE CHEESE BUTTER

Serves 2

Sometimes the best meals you can cook together take the least amount of time; this grilled porterhouse steak is an excellent example. Go to your local butcher shop and look for the most gorgeously marbled, thick-cut steak you can find. You shouldn't do too much to a great piece of meat—a light marinade with some garlic and fresh thyme enhances, instead of obscuring, the natural flavor.

One 2³⁄₄-inch-thick porterhouse steak (about 2¹⁄₂ pounds)
1 tablespoon kosher salt
1 teaspoon freshly ground black pepper
1 tablespoon chopped fresh thyme
6 cloves garlic, minced
¹⁄₄ cup extra-virgin olive oil
Blue Cheese Butter (recipe follows)

1. Rub the steak generously with the salt, pepper, thyme, and garlic. Place the steak in a deep dish and pour the olive oil over it. Cover and let the meat marinate for an hour in the refrigerator.

2. Preheat an indoor or outdoor grill to high heat.

3. Grill the steak for about 5 to 6 minutes on each side, until a meat thermometer inserted horizontally into the steak registers 120°F for rare. (The meat will continue cooking from the residual heat once it's off the grill.) Let the steak rest for 10 minutes on a cutting board; the temperature will increase to between 125°F and 128°F, about medium-rare. Slice the meat against the grain and serve with a pat of Blue Cheese Butter.

Meat, Poultry & Seafood Dishes

BLUE CHEESE BUTTER

Makes ⅓ cup of butter

3 tablespoons unsalted butter, softened

2 tablespoons crumbled blue cheese

¹/₂ teaspoon Worcestershire sauce

¹/₄ teaspoon freshly ground black pepper

1 anchovy fillet, finely minced (optional)

1. Stir together the butter, blue cheese, Worcestershire sauce, pepper, and anchovy fillet. Wrap the butter in plastic wrap and refrigerate for about 20 minutes to firm up.

BALSAMIC-GLAZED TURKEY MEAT LOAF

Serves 2, with leftovers

The key to life (and maybe even marital bliss) is balance: sometimes it's cookie dough for dinner, and sometimes it's this light and healthful balsamic-glazed turkey meat loaf. This leaner version is just as flavorful and moist as the traditional version made with beef and pork, thanks to the diced red peppers and fragrant spices of cumin and fennel seed. The tangy-sweet glaze of Worcestershire sauce, balsamic vinegar, and ketchup is sure to please grown-ups and kids alike.

2 tablespoons extra-virgin olive oil
³/₄ cup finely diced sweet yellow onion
1 cup diced red bell pepper
1 pound ground turkey
1 teaspoon kosher salt
¹/₂ teaspoon freshly ground black pepper
1 teaspoon dried thyme
¹/₂ teaspoon ground cumin
¹/₂ teaspoon fennel seeds
1 large egg, beaten
¹/₂ cup bread crumbs
¹/₄ cup ketchup
¹/₄ cup balsamic vinegar
3 tablespoons Worcestershire sauce

1. Preheat the oven to 350°F.

2. Heat the olive oil in a medium skillet over medium-high heat. Add the onions and sauté until softened and lightly browned, 5 to 6 minutes. Add the red bell peppers and sauté for 3 to 4 minutes until softened. Remove the skillet from the heat and let the vegetables cool.

3. Put the ground turkey in a large bowl; add the salt, pepper, thyme, cumin, and fennel seeds. Gently mix in the egg and the bread crumbs, taking care not to overwork the mixture. Mix in the cooked onions and peppers.

4. In a separate bowl, whisk together the ketchup, balsamic vinegar, and Worcestershire sauce. Add three quarters of the sauce mixture to the ground turkey, mixing it in until just combined.

5. Pat the meat loaf mixture into a parchment-lined loaf pan. Brush the remaining glaze on top of the meat loaf, and bake for 50 to 55 minutes. Let cool in the pan for 5 to 10 minutes before unmolding.

HOLIDAY RIB ROAST WITH THYME GRAVY

Serves 8

This high-heat, low-heat method for cooking a rib roast results in a nicely seared crust, with a perfectly tender and juicy interior all the way through. Have leftovers after the families have stuffed themselves at your table? Lucky you: Simply reheat thin slices of meat in the leftover gravy, and top with a little creamed horseradish for the tastiest hot roast beef sandwich.

FOR THE ROAST:

One 10-pound standing rib roast

6 medium carrots, peeled and cut into $^{1}/_{2}$-inch-thick coins

8 ribs celery, cut into $^{1}/_{4}$-inch-thick pieces

3 onions, cut into $^{1}/_{2}$-inch rings

3 bay leaves

5 cloves garlic, peeled

1 bottle dry white wine

Kosher salt and freshly ground black pepper

Leaves from 6 sprigs fresh thyme

2 tablespoons chopped fresh rosemary leaves

FOR THE GRAVY:

$1^{1}/_{4}$ cup drippings from the roast

2 tablespoons unsalted butter

$^{1}/_{2}$ cup flour

$1^{1}/_{2}$ teaspoons chopped fresh thyme

1 cup beef broth

$^{3}/_{4}$ cup half-and-half

Kosher salt and freshly ground black pepper

1. To make the roast, 2 hours before you intend to cook it, remove the roast from the refrigerator and allow it to come to room temperature.

2. Preheat the oven to 475°F.

3. Place the carrots, celery, onions, bay leaves, garlic, and wine in the bottom of a large, heavy-bottomed roasting pan fitted with a roasting rack.

4. Season the rib roast liberally with kosher salt and pepper (you'll need to use about 3 tablespoons of kosher salt and 1½ tablespoons of pepper, which seems like a lot, but isn't, considering the amount of meat). Sprinkle the thyme and rosemary on the roast, and place it on the roasting rack above the vegetables. Transfer the roasting pan to the oven, and cook the roast for 12 to 15 minutes, or until the meat develops a nice crust.

5. Reduce the temperature to 250°F, and continue roasting until a meat thermometer inserted into the center of the roast registers 130°F for medium-rare (about 2½ hours for a 10-pound roast).

6. Let the roast rest for at least 20 minutes before slicing. Meanwhile, prepare the gravy.

7. To make the gravy, strain the drippings from the roasting pan, discarding the vegetables, garlic, and bay leaf, and reserve. In a large saucepan over medium heat, add the butter and whisk until it has melted. Add the flour and cook for 2 minutes, stirring constantly with the whisk. Add the thyme, reserved drippings, beef broth, and half-and-half, and continue to stir until the mixture bubbles and thickens, about 10 to 12 minutes. Season to taste with salt and pepper.

8. Slice the meat, and serve with the gravy.

CORNMEAL-CRUSTED FRIED FISH FILLETS WITH HOMEMADE TARTAR SAUCE

Serves 2

Sometimes nothing will do except a big platter of fried goodness. Whenever the craving hits, try these fish fillets, which fry up in only about three minutes. The cornmeal keeps the fish extra crunchy, and the tartar sauce is so fresh and tart from the dill and capers, you won't ever go back to buying the bottled stuff again. (And psst . . . dipping the Buttermilk Onion Rings on page 169 in the tartar sauce is a splendid indulgence!)

> 1 large egg, beaten
> 1½ cups buttermilk
> ¼ cup cornmeal
> ⅔ cup flour
> 1½ teaspoons kosher salt
> 1½ teaspoons sweet paprika
> ½ teaspoon freshly ground black pepper
> 1 teaspoon cayenne
> 1 pound catfish fillets (defrosted, if frozen)
> Canola, vegetable, or peanut oil for frying
> Tartar Sauce (recipe follows)

1. Whisk the egg and buttermilk together in a shallow dish.

2. In another shallow dish, combine the cornmeal, flour, salt, paprika, black pepper, and cayenne. Dredge the fish fillets first in the buttermilk mixture and then in the seasoned flour. Shake off any excess and repeat until all the fish is evenly coated on both sides.

3. Heat 4 inches of oil in a deep pot until a deep-fat thermometer registers 360°F.

4. Fry the fish for 3 to 4 minutes, until the crust is golden brown, making sure the entire fillet is submerged in the oil. Drain on paper towels before serving with Tartar Sauce.

CORNMEAL-CRUSTED
FRIED FISH FILLETS WITH
HOMEMADE TARTAR SAUCE

TARTAR SAUCE

Makes about ³/₄ cup of sauce

¹/₂ **cup mayonnaise**

1 tablespoon capers, drained and chopped

1 tablespoon finely chopped dill pickle

1¹/₂ tablespoons chopped fresh dill, parsley, or tarragon

³/₄ **teaspoon Worcestershire sauce**

¹/₈ **teaspoon freshly ground black pepper**

2 tablespoons freshly squeezed lemon juice

1. Mix all the ingredients together in a small bowl and refrigerate until needed. The sauce will keep, covered and refrigerated, for 3 to 4 days.

Adventurous Palates

✤

MATTHEW AND JANEL BENNETT, CHEF-
OWNERS OF SYBARIS IN ALBANY, OREGON

Married: July 25, 1998

C an we talk about the chicken feet?" Matthew Bennett asks his wife, Janel.

"Oh, boy, the chicken feet!" laughs Janel. "But won't that *discourage* people from wanting to try new foods?"

Janel and Matthew are co-owners of Sybaris, an Oregon bistro focusing on the flavors of the Northwest. When not at work, they love to eat and travel, making sure to always taste unfamiliar or fabled ingredients. So several years ago when they were invited to cook at the James Beard House in New York City, they were determined to eat as much regional food as possible, including the kind of "adventurous" dim sum they couldn't find in Albany.

The couple took a chance in Chinatown and walked into the first crowded food spot they saw with no obvious tourists or Westerners inside. Janel and Matthew quickly found themselves at the center of attention, as tables of locals watched the couple decline plate after plate of familiar foods in exchange for more adventurous dishes (even as their waiter tried to discourage them from doing so).

"There was a lot of signing and gesturing," Matthew says of their limited communication with the waiters. "But when we noticed we were the only people not eating chicken feet, they really tried to talk us out of it!"

Undeterred, they ordered the chicken feet, knowing they could both manage to eat at least one. The entire restaurant fell silent as all of the diners turned and watched.

"It was pretty bad," Matthew remembers, laughing. "Once you got underneath the crispy coating, there was a lot of cartilage and bone. We didn't want to be insulting, so we just nodded and politely smiled."

Despite the experience, Janel and Matthew say they still love traveling and trying "scary" food. They even keep mental lists of foods to check off, including the jellyfish they recently sampled at a Japanese restaurant in San Francisco.

"Travel makes you a better cook," Matthew continues, "and, if nothing else, a better storyteller! Taste everything, and learn to apply the tricks of the region to any dish. That's how you make a dish your own."

ADVICE FOR NEWLYWEDS: *"When traveling, ask cooks and servers where to eat instead of your concierge. Go behind restaurants where the cooks are out back smoking and ask them where they go for the specialties of that area. We've never been led astray that way."*

—*Matthew*

FAVORITE THING IN THE KITCHEN: *"An inexpensive stainless steel Chinese cleaver. Most home cooks don't faithfully sharpen their knives. Those people are better served with a couple of $5 cleavers and good paring knives, rather than a pricey, professional knife."*

—*Matthew*

PANCETTA-WRAPPED PORK WITH GORGONZOLA SAUCE

Serves 2 to 4

This pancetta-wrapped pork tenderloin looks upscale, but it is one of the easiest recipes in this cookbook—perfect for a Friday date-night when you don't want to spend much effort making dinner. The rich Gorgonzola sauce is accented with herbs and a bit of heat from the red pepper flakes. Try serving this dish with creamy mashed potatoes—the little crevices catch and cradle every bit of the lovely cheese sauce.

3 cloves garlic, finely chopped
1 tablespoon chopped fresh sage
1 tablespoon extra-virgin olive oil
³/₄ teaspoon kosher salt
¹/₄ teaspoon freshly ground black pepper
1 pound pork tenderloin
5 thin slices pancetta
Gorgonzola Sauce (recipe follows)

1. Combine the garlic, sage, olive oil, salt, and pepper in a small bowl, and whisk to combine. Rub the mixture over the pork tenderloin. Cover the meat and marinate for 1 hour (or overnight) in the refrigerator.

2. Preheat the oven to 425°F.

3. Place the tenderloin in a roasting pan and drape the slices of pancetta over the top, slightly overlapping each slice. Cook for 16 to 20 minutes (16 minutes for medium-rare, 20 minutes for medium-well), or until a meat thermometer inserted into the center of the pork registers 140°F. Let the pork rest for at least 10 minutes before slicing (the temperature of the pork will rise about 10 degrees higher during this time). Spoon the Gorgonzola Sauce over the sliced tenderloin and serve.

GORGONZOLA SAUCE

Makes ²/₃ cup of sauce

> 1 tablespoon unsalted butter
> 1 tablespoon flour
> ¹/₃ cup heavy cream
> 2 tablespoons dry white wine
> 2 tablespoons chicken stock
> 3 ounces Gorgonzola
> 1 tablespoon snipped fresh chives
> ¹/₄ teaspoon chopped fresh thyme
> Small pinch of red pepper flakes (optional)

1. In a small saucepan over medium-high heat combine the butter and flour and stir for 2 minutes. Add the cream, wine, chicken stock, Gorgonzola, chives, thyme, and red pepper flakes, and stir until the sauce reduces and thickens slightly, about 5 to 6 minutes.

CHEDDAR CHEESE GRITS WITH SHRIMP AND BACON GRAVY

Serves 2

These shrimp and cheddar cheese grits are a bowlful of love on a blustery winter day. This is pure indulgent comfort food—the kind our souls crave on nights in and best eaten nestled under a big blanket with a good book.

1 cup whole milk
1¼ cups water
½ cup quick-cooking grits or polenta
2 tablespoons unsalted butter
¾ cup (about 3 ounces) shredded sharp cheddar cheese
1 tablespoon vegetable oil
3 strips bacon, cut into bite-size pieces
⅓ cup diced red bell pepper
⅓ cup diced yellow bell pepper
2 tablespoons chopped fresh parsley
⅓ cup minced green onions (about 2)
½ pound large shrimp, shelled and deveined
2 tablespoons flour
1 cup chicken stock
Kosher salt and freshly ground black pepper
Hot sauce (optional)
Lemon wedges (optional)

1. In a large saucepan over high heat, combine the milk and water and bring to a boil. Lower the heat to medium and add the grits to the pan. Stir the grits with a whisk for 15 to 20 minutes, until they are smooth and any lumps have dissolved. Stir in the butter and cheddar. Set aside and keep warm.

2. Heat the oil in a medium skillet over medium-high heat. Add the bacon and cook until crisp, then remove it with a slotted spoon, leaving the drippings in the pan. Set the bacon aside on a paper towel to drain.

CHEDDAR CHEESE
GRITS WITH SHRIMP
AND BACON GRAVY

3. Add the red and yellow bell pepper, parsley, and green onions to the skillet and cook until tender, 3 to 4 minutes. Add the shrimp and cook until they turn pink and opaque, about 2 minutes. Stir in the flour and cook for 1 minute. Then whisk in the chicken stock and wait for the sauce to bubble and thicken, about 2 minutes. Season to taste with salt and pepper.

4. Spoon the shrimp and gravy over the grits, and sprinkle with the reserved bacon. Serve with hot sauce or a squeeze of lemon, if desired.

EXTRA-CHEESY CLASSIC LASAGNA

Serves 2, with leftovers

There are few more soul-satisfying things to eat than a big plate of piping hot, cheesy lasagna, layered with a robustly flavored meat sauce. This recipe will serve two hearty appetites, and you'll also have enough for leftovers the next day.

FOR THE RAGÙ:

3 tablespoons extra-virgin olive oil

3 ounces pancetta or bacon, cut into ¼-inch dice

1½ cups (about 1 large) finely diced sweet yellow onion

4 cloves garlic, finely chopped

¾ pound ground beef

½ pound sweet Italian sausage, casings removed

1½ teaspoons kosher salt

½ teaspoon freshly ground black pepper

1 teaspoon chopped fresh oregano

1½ teaspoons dried marjoram

¼ teaspoon red pepper flakes (optional)

One 28-ounce can crushed tomatoes

¼ cup tomato paste

1 cup packed fresh basil, torn into small pieces

FOR THE RICOTTA FILLING:

20 ounces whole-milk ricotta

6 ounces frozen spinach, defrosted and squeezed dry

1 large egg

½ teaspoon kosher salt

¼ teaspoon ground nutmeg (optional)

FOR THE LASAGNA:

10 lasagna noodles, parboiled for about 9 minutes and drained

2½ cups grated mozzarella, divided

1½ cups grated Parmesan, divided

1. Preheat the oven to 375°F.

2. To make the ragù, heat the olive oil in a large skillet over medium heat. Add the pancetta and cook until brown and crisp, about 2 minutes. Add the onions and cook until they soften and turn golden brown, about 7 minutes. Add the garlic, ground beef, sausage, salt, pepper, oregano, marjoram, and red pepper flakes. Brown the meat, breaking up the large pieces with a spatula. Add the crushed tomatoes, tomato paste, and basil. Lower the heat to medium-low, cover the skillet, and simmer the sauce for at least 15 minutes or up to an hour, if you have time. (The longer you simmer the sauce, the softer and rounder the flavors become.)

3. To make the ricotta filling, in a large bowl, add all the ingredients and stir to combine.

4. To assemble the lasagna, in a 13-by-9-inch baking dish, lay 4 cooked lasagna noodles down evenly, overlapping them slightly. Ladle one third of the ragù over the noodles, using the back of the ladle to smooth the sauce evenly over the pasta. Add half the ricotta mixture on top of the ragù, then sprinkle with $3/4$ cup of mozzarella and $1/2$ cup of Parmesan. Add 3 lasagna noodles for the second layer and repeat with the ragù, ricotta, mozzarella, and Parmesan. Lay the last 3 lasagna noodles on top and cover with the last third of the ragù and the remaining mozzarella and Parmesan.

5. Cover the pan with aluminum foil and bake for 30 minutes. Remove the foil and continue baking for 15 to 20 minutes longer, or until the top layer of cheese is golden brown.

6. Let the lasagna cool for 10 minutes before serving, so it has a chance to firm up slightly in the pan.

FALL-APART POT ROAST

Serves 2, with leftovers

Many of us love a good, hearty pot roast. This recipe is incredibly flavorful from the thyme and oregano, and the combination of honey, balsamic vinegar, and Dijon mustard lends depth to this family favorite. Don't let the lengthy ingredient list deter you—most of the ingredients just get thrown in the pot with the beef, leaving you both plenty of time to negotiate dessert!

> 3 tablespoons flour
> $1\frac{1}{2}$ tablespoons kosher salt
> 1 teaspoon freshly ground black pepper
> $2\frac{1}{2}$ pounds chuck roast
> 2 tablespoons extra-virgin olive oil
> 1 large sweet yellow onion, chopped
> 3 cloves garlic, chopped
> 1 cup dry red wine
> 2 cups low-sodium beef broth
> 2 beef bouillon cubes
> 3 sprigs fresh thyme
> 3 sprigs fresh oregano
> 2 bay leaves
> 3 tablespoons tomato paste
> 1 tablespoon honey
> 3 tablespoons balsamic vinegar
> 3 tablespoons Dijon mustard
> 3 carrots, peeled and cut into bite-size pieces
> $\frac{3}{4}$ pound Yukon Gold potatoes, quartered
> 8 ounces cremini mushrooms, halved

1. In a large, deep dish, combine the flour, salt, and pepper. Dredge the chuck roast in the seasoned flour.

2. Heat the olive oil in a large skillet over medium-high heat. Brown the meat for 5 minutes per side, until it is nicely seared. In a large, heavy-bottomed pot or Dutch oven, combine the onion, garlic, wine, broth, bouillon cubes, thyme, oregano, bay leaves,

tomato paste, honey, balsamic vinegar, Dijon mustard, and carrots, along with the meat. Bring everything to a simmer, partially covered, over medium heat.

3. Cook for 2 hours and 15 minutes, then add the potatoes and mushrooms. (The liquid should have been reduced by almost half at this point. If it has reduced too much, add a little water.) Simmer for another hour, partially covered, until the braising liquid has achieved a thick, saucelike consistency. Pierce a potato to check doneness: if it is still too firm, simmer for another 15 minutes. Remove the meat carefully from the pot (it will be almost falling apart at this point, so use two spatulas to lift the meat out of the pot and position the cutting board nearby.) Slice the meat and serve alongside the vegetables, with the sauce spooned over the top.

ULTRA-CRISPY SECRET FRIED CHICKEN

Serves 3 to 4

Fried chicken is a perennial favorite—especially when it's well seasoned, with a delicious, crunchy crust. The secret ingredient? Plain soda water, which makes the crust extra crispy! The chicken needs to be dry-rubbed at least 8 hours, so start the night before. And if you want to prepare the recipe several hours before serving, this chicken holds up beautifully—the crust will still be amazingly crunchy.

FOR THE DRY RUB:
> 2 tablespoons garlic salt
> 1 tablespoon freshly ground black pepper
> 1½ tablespoons paprika
> ½ teaspoon cayenne
> 4 pounds assorted chicken parts (about 8 pieces: legs, thighs, breasts, wings)

FOR THE BATTER:
> 1½ cups plain soda water, such as Pellegrino
> 1 cup flour
> 1 tablespoon hot sauce

FOR THE SEASONED FLOUR:
> 2 cups flour
> 2 teaspoons kosher salt
> 2 teaspoons freshly ground black pepper
>
> Vegetable, canola, or peanut oil for frying

1. To make the dry rub, combine the garlic salt, black pepper, paprika, and cayenne in a small bowl and rub the mixture evenly over the chicken pieces. Place the chicken in a pan, cover, and refrigerate overnight.

2. To make the batter, in a shallow pan, whisk the soda water completely into the flour before adding the hot sauce. Stir to combine.

3. To make the seasoned flour, in another shallow pan, combine the flour, salt, and pepper. Dip each piece of chicken first in the batter and then in the seasoned flour. Repeat until all the chicken pieces are battered and coated in flour.

4. Heat your deep fryer to 360°F (or use a deep pot, fill it a third of the way with oil, and heat the oil until a deep-fat thermometer registers 360°F).

5. Working in small batches, fry each piece of chicken for 8 to 9 minutes on one side, then flip and fry for 10 minutes on the other side. Make sure the oil heats back up to 360°F before you start frying the next batch. Drain the fried chicken on paper towels, and keep the pieces warm in the oven as you finish frying.

RACK OF LAMB WITH SOUR CHERRIES, CAULIFLOWER, AND CAPERS

Serves 2

You may think that rack of lamb is something best left to fancy restaurants, but all you need is a meat thermometer to get perfect results every time. This simple sour cherry, cauliflower, and caper pan sauce comes together while the lamb is roasting, and the sweet/tart/earthy/tangy flavors play off one another in a most beguiling fashion. My inspiration to combine dried fruit, cauliflower, and capers came from Jean-Georges Vongerichten, one of the greatest chefs of our time.

FOR THE LAMB:

$1\frac{1}{4}$-pound rack of lamb (4 to 8 chops, depending on size)

$\frac{1}{2}$ teaspoon kosher salt

$\frac{1}{4}$ teaspoon freshly ground black pepper

1 tablespoon extra-virgin olive oil

FOR THE SAUCE:

$\frac{1}{3}$ cup sour cherries

$\frac{1}{4}$ cup dry red wine

4 tablespoons ($\frac{1}{2}$ stick) unsalted butter, divided

$\frac{1}{2}$ cup cauliflower florets

$\frac{1}{8}$ teaspoon freshly ground black pepper

$\frac{1}{4}$ cup capers

1 tablespoon honey

1 teaspoon freshly squeezed lemon juice

1. Preheat the oven to 400°F. Pat the rack of lamb dry, and sprinkle with the salt and pepper.

2. Heat the olive oil in a large ovenproof pan over medium-high heat. Brown the lamb for 2 minutes per side.

3. Place the pan in the oven and roast for approximately 15 to 20 minutes, or until a meat thermometer inserted in the center registers 130°F for medium-rare.

4. While the lamb is roasting, make the sauce. Place the sour cherries in a small bowl with the red wine to plump for a few minutes. Meanwhile, in a medium skillet over medium-high heat, melt 3 tablespoons of the butter. Add the cauliflower and cook until golden brown, about 3 to 4 minutes. Add the pepper, then add the capers, sour cherries, and wine. Let the wine reduce for about 2 minutes, then add the honey, lemon juice, and the remaining butter.

5. Let the lamb rest for 5 to 10 minutes before slicing. Spoon the cauliflower sauce over the top of the lamb chops and serve.

ITALIAN GRANDMOTHER MEATBALLS

Serves 2, with leftovers

These are meatballs any little old Italian grandmother would approve of! Italians typically use a combination of three types of meat for meatballs: beef (for its meaty flavor punch), pork (for its fat content), and veal (for its mild, sweet taste). You can serve the meatballs on spaghetti, the way we love them in America, or try them on polenta, which is more authentic. Cap off your Italian feast with the perfect soundtrack and a bottle of wine (or two!).

FOR THE MEATBALLS:

$^1/_4$ cup whole milk

1 cup day-old cubed bread, crusts removed

$^1/_3$ pound ground veal

$^1/_3$ pound ground pork

$^3/_4$ pound ground beef

1 large egg

$^1/_3$ cup grated Parmesan or pecorino, plus more for garnish

3 tablespoons chopped fresh parsley, plus more for garnish

$^3/_4$ teaspoon kosher salt

$^1/_2$ teaspoon freshly ground black pepper

2 teaspoons chopped fresh oregano

2 cloves garlic, finely diced

Small pinch of red pepper flakes (optional)

$^1/_4$ cup extra-virgin olive oil for frying

FOR THE TOMATO SAUCE:

$^1/_3$ cup extra-virgin olive oil

$^3/_4$ cup diced sweet yellow onion

4 cloves garlic, finely minced

One 28-ounce can crushed tomatoes

3 tablespoons tomato paste

$^3/_4$ cup fresh basil leaves, torn

Kosher salt and freshly ground black pepper

1. To make the meatballs, pour the milk into a small bowl and soak the bread cubes for 2 minutes.

2. In a large bowl, combine the soaked bread, veal, pork, beef, egg, Parmesan, parsley, salt, pepper, oregano, garlic, and red pepper flakes. Mix together lightly and form into balls measuring about 2 inches in diameter. Don't overmix the meat or compress the meatballs too tightly in your hands, as the meat will become tough.

3. Heat the oil in a large skillet over medium-high heat. Fry the meatballs, taking care not to overcrowd the pan (you may have to cook them in two batches), until they are deeply browned on all sides, about 8 to 10 minutes total. (The meatballs will continue cooking in the tomato sauce.)

4. To make the tomato sauce, heat the olive oil in a large skillet over medium heat. Add the onions and cook for 7 to 8 minutes, or until golden brown. Add the garlic, crushed tomatoes, tomato paste, and basil. Season to taste with salt and pepper and bring the sauce to a simmer. Place the meatballs in the tomato sauce and simmer for 25 to 30 minutes. Serve the meatballs and sauce garnished with a little extra parsley and Parmesan.

Wild at Heart

❧

STEVEN RINELLA, AUTHOR OF *AMERICAN BUFFALO* AND *THE SCAVENGER'S GUIDE TO HAUTE CUISINE*, AND HIS WIFE, KATIE FINCH

Married: July 12, 2008

Perhaps no couple can make a greater case for establishing harmony in a kitchen where there once was none than Katie Finch and Steven Rinella. The famously opposite couple—she's a chic New York publicist, and he's an avid hunter and outdoorsman—met when Katie promoted Steven's first book, *The Scavenger's Guide to Haute Cuisine*, a depiction of his yearlong quest to hunt, fish, forage, prepare, and cook the ingredients for a five-day, forty-five-course feast. Despite the fact that Katie had never cooked a meal, let alone stalked and butchered one, their second date turned into a lifetime: Steven fell head over heels and left his remote Alaskan cabin for an elegant brownstone and Katie's sophisticated New York lifestyle.

He didn't abandon his adventurous habits, though. A man who thrives in challenging terrain doesn't cave in the face of a concrete jungle. Instead, he adapted. Steven built an extensive culinary garden in their Brooklyn backyard, stocked the empty kitchen with tools and cookware, and converted a walk-in closet to accommodate an oversize freezer chest stocked to the brim with wild game.

"She was a little freaked out to have all these guns and dead animals around the house," Steven laughs. "It was challenging at first because I'm a huge proponent of eating at home, and everyone in New York eats out. So I started cooking, and now she's really open to it."

"There is a *saw* hanging in our kitchen!" Katie laughs, but she is quick to admit that Steven's culinary skills have influenced how she thinks about food. "I've always been pretty intimidated by cooking and didn't have a lot of patience for it. Now I mix cocktails and watch him cook."

Steven worked hard, wooing Katie with elaborate meals such as grilled caribou steak and Caesar salad with romaine hearts; wild boar ribs and coleslaw; and seared smoked venison, thoughtfully varying dishes and paying attention to what she responded to. Now Katie—who had dabbled in vegetarianism—refuses restaurant meat, preferring Steven's wild game to factory or farm-raised meats. She has even ventured into cooking for the first time, taking cues from Steven and learning to grill salmon and prepare simple side dishes.

Katie also finds ways to return his culinary generosity, creating a giant spreadsheet organizing the contents of the freezer, from antelope shank to eel to rockfish to squirrel.

"If you care about each other, you find ways to reciprocate," Steven says. "Katie sets a beautiful table, keeps me company in the kitchen, and eats what I cook. What more could I ask for?"

ADVICE FOR NEWLYWEDS: *"Stay open to new ideas and be willing to hear your spouse's perspective. With an open mind, your lives together become much more pleasurable."*

—Katie

FAVORITE THINGS IN THE KITCHEN: *"Dreams of a giant mixer."*

—Katie

"The meat grinder."

—Steven

SUPER BOWL CHILI

Serves 4 to 6

This chili recipe combines chunks of supremely tender braised beef with a mix of ground beef, sausage, and beer. It has a bit of a kick from the dried ancho chilies, but it's mild enough to be a crowd pleaser. Serve big bowls of this chili with sour cream, grated cheese, sliced avocado, chopped red onion, tortilla chips, and your favorite fiery hot sauce on the side, so your friends can tailor their bowl to their tastes. Even if they aren't football fans, they'll come for the chili! This recipe can easily be doubled for a bigger party.

3 dried ancho chilies, seeded and stemmed

1$\frac{1}{4}$ cups boiling-hot water

4 strips bacon, cut into $\frac{1}{4}$-inch dice

2 tablespoons vegetable oil, divided

1 large onion, cut into $\frac{1}{4}$-inch dice

3 cloves garlic, finely minced

1 pound beef stew meat, cut into $\frac{1}{2}$-inch pieces

Kosher salt and freshly ground black pepper

$\frac{1}{2}$ pound lean ground beef

1 pound mild Italian sausage, casings removed

One 28-ounce can crushed tomatoes

One 6-ounce can tomato paste

One 12-ounce bottle dark beer

3 teaspoons ground cumin

2 tablespoons chili powder

1$\frac{1}{2}$ tablespoons sweet paprika

1$\frac{1}{2}$ tablespoons dried oregano

1 teaspoon red pepper flakes

2$\frac{1}{2}$ tablespoons Worcestershire sauce

2 tablespoons liquid smoke

1 beef bouillon cube

One 14-ounce can cannellini beans

1. Soak the ancho chilies in the hot water for 20 minutes, until softened. In a blender, purée the chilies with the liquid. Pour the liquid into a large, heavy-bottomed pot or Dutch oven, and set aside.

2. In a medium skillet over medium heat, cook the bacon until crisp, about 3 to 4 minutes. Add 1 tablespoon of the vegetable oil and the onions and garlic to the skillet with the bacon. Cook until onions are softened and golden brown, 10 to 12 minutes. Transfer the onion mixture to the pot with the puréed chilies and do not wash the skillet.

3. Season the beef stew meat with salt and pepper to taste. Add the remaining vegetable oil to the skillet, and brown the stew meat on all sides, about 5 minutes total. Transfer the beef to the pot, then brown the ground beef and sausage in the same skillet, about 5 minutes. Transfer the meat to the pot.

4. Add the crushed tomatoes, tomato paste, beer, cumin, chili powder, paprika, oregano, red pepper flakes, Worcestershire sauce, liquid smoke, bouillon cube, and cannellini beans to the pot and simmer, partially covered, over medium-low heat for 1 hour and 30 minutes, stirring every 20 minutes or so.

5. The chili can be made up to 2 days ahead; store covered in the refrigerator.

BACKYARD BARBECUE
MILE-HIGH BURGERS AND
BUTTERMILK ONION RINGS

BACKYARD BARBECUE MILE-HIGH BURGERS AND BUTTERMILK ONION RINGS

Serves 2

For the best burger you've got to start with the best meat—preferably freshly ground, dry-aged or grass-fed beef. A local farmer I interviewed recommended adding one egg yolk per pound of ground beef—it's that extra little dab of fat from the yolk that will make your burger super special. These burgers are fantastic served with a side of my golden-hued onion rings, which are crispy in texture and rendered sweeter by a short soak in flavored buttermilk. Be sure to slice the onions as thinly as you possibly can—$^1/_{10}$ of an inch thick or less—either with a very sharp knife or using a mandoline for best results.

FOR THE BURGERS:

- 1 pound of the freshest, best-quality ground beef you have access to, preferably 80 percent lean
- 1 egg yolk
- 2 cloves garlic, finely minced
- 1 teaspoon Worcestershire sauce
- 3 tablespoons crumbled blue cheese, divided
- $^1/_2$ teaspoon kosher salt
- $^1/_4$ teaspoon freshly ground black pepper
- 1 tablespoon extra-virgin olive oil
- 4 strips thick-cut bacon

FOR THE ONIONS AND MUSHROOMS:

- 2 tablespoons unsalted butter, softened
- $^1/_2$ medium red onion, thinly sliced
- 5 ounces sliced cremini mushrooms
- 1 tablespoon sherry vinegar
- $^1/_2$ teaspoon Worcestershire sauce
- 2 teaspoons honey
- 3 tablespoons heavy cream
- $^1/_2$ teaspoon chopped fresh thyme
- Pinch of kosher salt and freshly ground black pepper

2 potato buns

2 tablespoons Garlic Mayonnaise (page 46) or regular mayonnaise

1 cup loosely packed arugula

2 slices tomato, preferably heirloom

Buttermilk Onion Rings (recipe follows)

Ketchup and mustard

1. To make the burgers, in a large bowl combine the ground beef, egg yolk, garlic, and Worcestershire sauce, mixing until just combined. Divide the meat into quarters and flatten into patties about 2 inches thick. Place half of the blue cheese on each of 2 patties and top each with the remaining patties, pressing the edges together with your fingers to seal the cheese inside. Sprinkle the salt and pepper on the outside of each burger.

2. Heat the olive oil in a small skillet over medium-high heat, and cook the bacon for 3 to 4 minutes, or until crisp. Drain the bacon on a paper towel, leaving the drippings in the skillet.

3. To make the onions, melt the butter in the skillet. Add the onions and cook until they are soft and golden brown, about 7 to 8 minutes. (If you like your onions extra-sweet and jammy, caramelize them by cooking them over low heat for about 45 minutes, stirring occasionally.) Add the mushrooms and cook for 5 to 6 minutes, or until browned. Stir in the sherry vinegar, Worcestershire sauce, honey, cream, and thyme, stirring for another 1 to 2 minutes, or until the cream reduces slightly. Season with salt and pepper. Remove the onions and mushrooms from the heat and set aside.

4. In a hot cast-iron skillet or over direct heat on a grill, cook the burgers for about 4 to 5 minutes per side for medium-rare.

5. To assemble the burgers, butter and toast the buns, and spread them with garlic mayonnaise. Place a small handful of arugula on the top bun and add one slice of tomato, two bacon strips, and a heaping spoonful of the onion and mushroom mixture. Repeat for the other bun. When the burgers are cooked, place them on the bottom bun. Serve with Buttermilk Onion Rings and ketchup and mustard on the side.

BUTTERMILK ONION RINGS

Serves 2

> 1 medium sweet onion, very thinly sliced
>
> 2 tablespoons hot sauce
>
> 1 teaspoon plus 1 tablespoon garlic salt
>
> 1 teaspoon freshly ground black pepper, divided
>
> 2 cups buttermilk
>
> 2 cups flour
>
> 1 teaspoon sweet paprika
>
> 1 quart vegetable, canola, or peanut oil for frying

1. In a large mixing bowl, combine the onions, hot sauce, 1 teaspoon of the garlic salt, and ½ teaspoon of the pepper. Pour in the buttermilk and press down on the onions to make sure most of them are submerged. Cover the bowl and refrigerate for 2 hours.

2. In a shallow bowl or large dish, combine the flour with the remaining garlic salt, the paprika, and the remaining pepper. Dredge the onions in the seasoned flour evenly and shake off any excess.

3. Heat the oil in a large, deep pot until it registers 360°F on a deep-fat thermometer.

4. Fry the onions in three batches, turning them with a pair of tongs so they cook evenly and turn golden brown, about 3 minutes per batch. Remove the onion rings from the oil and drain on paper towels. Taste for seasoning and add a little extra salt if desired.

PAPRIKA-SPICED HUNGARIAN BEEF GOULASH

Serves 2, with leftovers

Back in the '60s and '70s, Hungarian beef goulash was quite the fashionable dish in America. This recipe, fragrant with paprika and caraway, is inspired by the beef stew many of us grew up eating at our mothers' tables. Why not continue the family tradition and cook up this hearty classic for dinner tonight?

3 tablespoons extra-virgin olive oil

2 strips bacon, cut into $^1/_2$-inch pieces

1 large sweet yellow onion, thinly sliced

3 cloves garlic, minced

$1^1/_2$ pounds beef stew meat (such as chuck roast), cut into $1^1/_2$-inch cubes

1 teaspoon kosher salt

$^1/_2$ teaspoon freshly ground black pepper

2 tablespoons flour

1 red bell pepper, finely diced

$^1/_2$ pound cremini mushrooms, quartered

1 tablespoon dark brown sugar

1 teaspoon caraway seeds

$1^1/_2$ tablespoons sweet Hungarian paprika

1 teaspoon dried marjoram

1 bay leaf

One 6-ounce can tomato paste

One 15-ounce can crushed tomatoes

1 cup low-sodium beef broth

1 cup dry white wine

$^1/_2$ pound (about 3 medium) Yukon Gold potatoes, cut into quarters

$^1/_2$ cup sour cream

Chopped parsley, for garnish

1. Heat the olive oil in a large skillet over medium-high heat. Add the bacon and cook until crisp, about 3 minutes. Remove the bacon pieces with a slotted spoon and transfer to a large, deep pot, leaving the drippings in the pan. Cook the onions in the drippings until they turn golden, 7 to 8 minutes. Add the garlic and cook for another minute. Transfer the onions to the pot with the bacon.

2. Sprinkle the beef with the salt and pepper. Place the flour on a large dish and dredge the meat in the flour. Cook the beef in the skillet for 2 to 3 minutes per side, or until the meat is brown and crusty. Transfer the meat to the pot, along with the red bell pepper, mushrooms, brown sugar, caraway seeds, paprika, marjoram, bay leaf, tomato paste, crushed tomatoes, broth, and wine.

3. Simmer the goulash for 1½ hours, covered, over medium-low heat. Add the potatoes and sour cream, and continue simmering, uncovered, for another 45 minutes, or until the meat is fork-tender and the potatoes are cooked through.

4. To serve, ladle the goulash into 2 bowls and garnish with parsley.

CHICKEN POTPIES WITH
CHEDDAR-THYME CRUSTS

CHICKEN POTPIES WITH CHEDDAR-THYME CRUSTS

Serves 2

My husband is not a fussy guy: for his birthday meal, all he requested was chicken potpie and an ice cream cake. So I made him the best damn chicken potpie I'd ever made for anyone. The smile on his face when he broke into that flaky, cheesy crust and spooned up the creamy chicken filling is something I'll always remember. I hope you'll both love this recipe as much as we do.

FOR THE FILLING:

3 strips bacon, diced

¾ cup diced onions

1 tablespoon vegetable or extra-virgin olive oil

⅓ cup diced carrots

¾ cup (about 2½ ounces) diced cremini mushrooms

½ teaspoon kosher salt

¼ teaspoon freshly ground black pepper

1½ teaspoons dried marjoram

½ teaspoon chopped fresh rosemary leaves

¼ teaspoon paprika

2 tablespoons unsalted butter

2 tablespoons flour

⅓ cup heavy cream

⅔ cup low-sodium chicken stock

1½ cups diced, cooked chicken

½ cup frozen peas (do not defrost)

FOR THE CRUST:

1 sheet puff pastry, defrosted

1 egg yolk

2 tablespoons whole milk

¼ cup grated sharp cheddar

⅛ teaspoon freshly ground black pepper

1 teaspoon chopped fresh thyme

1. Preheat the oven to 375°F.

2. To make the filling, in a large skillet, cook the bacon over medium-high heat until crisp, 3 to 4 minutes. Add the onions and oil to the skillet with the bacon, and cook the onions for 8 to 9 minutes, or until they are golden brown. Add the carrots and mushrooms, and cook for 4 minutes. Stir in the salt, pepper, marjoram, rosemary, and paprika. Add the butter. When the butter melts, stir in the flour. Add the cream and chicken stock, and let the liquids simmer for 2 to 3 minutes, until they reduce slightly. Add the chicken and the frozen peas, and turn off the heat.

3. Transfer the filling into two large ramekins or a small casserole dish.

4. To make the crust, unfold the puff pastry sheet, place it over the ramekins, and trim any overhang.

5. In a small bowl, add the egg yolk and milk and whisk to combine.

6. Lightly brush the top of each potpie with a bit of the beaten egg yolk mixture. With a knife, cut a few vents in the puff pastry to let the steam escape.

7. In another small bowl, mix the cheddar, pepper, and thyme. Distribute the cheddar mixture evenly over the top of each potpie. Place the ramekins on a baking sheet.

8. Bake the potpies for 30 to 35 minutes, or until the pastry is golden and the filling is bubbling.

BOURBON-GLAZED BABY BACK RIBS WITH SWEET-AND-SMOKY BARBECUE SAUCE

Serves 2

This recipe may look a little lengthy, but the process is very simple. The ribs are marinated overnight with a chopped onion, garlic salt, pepper, cola (yes, cola!), and beer. The pan of ribs is then transferred directly into the oven, and then you have nothing more to do than whisk together the two sauces. The Sweet-and-Smoky Barbecue Sauce is a great one to keep around for chicken and steaks—once you see how easy it is to make your own sauce, you'll never buy the bottled version again!

FOR THE RIBS:

1 rack (about 2½ pounds) baby back ribs

1 tablespoon garlic salt

1 teaspoon freshly ground black pepper

3 tablespoons packed dark brown sugar

2 tablespoons Dijon mustard

1 cup cola (not diet)

One 12-ounce bottle amber beer

1 large sweet yellow onion, cut into ¼-inch-thick rounds

FOR THE BASTING SAUCE:

3 tablespoons packed dark brown sugar

¼ teaspoon cayenne (optional)

3 tablespoons bourbon or whiskey

¼ cup ketchup

2 tablespoons apple cider vinegar

2 tablespoons Dijon mustard

1 teaspoon liquid smoke

Sweet-and-Smoky Barbecue Sauce (recipe follows)

1. To make the ribs, place them in a large ovenproof pan. Rub the garlic salt, pepper, brown sugar, and mustard over the ribs. Pour the cola and beer over the ribs, add the onions, and cover the pan tightly with foil. Marinate in the refrigerator for at least 3 hours (preferably overnight).

2.	Preheat the oven to 300°F.

3.	Transfer the pan (still covered with the foil) directly into the oven and bake the ribs for 3 hours. Remove the foil and discard the cola, beer, and onions.

4.	Preheat the broiler.

5.	To make the basting sauce, whisk together all the ingredients in a small bowl. Baste the ribs with half the sauce, and broil them for 5 minutes, until they are slightly charred. Baste the ribs generously again with the remaining sauce, and broil for 3 to 5 more minutes. Serve with a side of the Sweet-and-Smoky Barbecue Sauce.

SWEET-AND-SMOKY BARBECUE SAUCE

Makes about 1¾ cups of sauce

> 1 cup ketchup
>
> 2 tablespoons molasses
>
> ¼ cup apple cider vinegar
>
> ¼ cup Worcestershire sauce
>
> 3 tablespoons dark brown sugar
>
> 2 tablespoons Dijon mustard
>
> 1 teaspoon liquid smoke
>
> ½ teaspoon garlic powder
>
> ½ teaspoon freshly ground black pepper

1.	In a large bowl, whisk together all the ingredients. The sauce will keep, covered, in the refrigerator for up to 1 week.

BOURBON-GLAZED BABY
BACK RIBS WITH SWEET-AND-
SMOKY BARBECUE SAUCE

BRAISED SHORT RIBS WITH SALSA VERDE AND HORSERADISH CREAM

Serves 2 to 4

Braised short ribs aren't difficult to make, but it's probably a dish more fitting for weekends or special occasions, when you both have a bit more time to relax and give the pot a quick peek every half hour. The lemon, lime, and parsley in the salsa keep the flavors fresh and lively, while the capers and anchovies give it a pungent dose of salt and acidity that a hearty dish like this needs. I recommend serving these tender short ribs on a bed of sweet and buttery mashed yams.

FOR THE SHORT RIBS:

2 teaspoons kosher salt

1 teaspoon freshly ground black pepper

3$^{1}/_{2}$ pounds bone-in short ribs

2 tablespoons extra-virgin olive oil

4 carrots, sliced into $^{1}/_{4}$-inch coins

5 ribs celery, finely diced

2 medium onions, finely diced

2 tablespoons balsamic vinegar

2 cups full-bodied red wine

1 quart low-sodium beef broth

1 beef bouillon cube

1 sprig fresh rosemary

1 teaspoon chopped fresh thyme

2 teaspoons dried marjoram

2 bay leaves

4 cloves garlic, finely minced

2 tablespoons dark brown sugar

> **Juice of 1 large lemon (about 2 tablespoons)**
> **Juice of 1 large lime (about 1$^1/_2$ tablespoons)**
> **$^1/_2$ cup packed fresh parsley**
> **$^1/_4$ cup extra-virgin olive oil**
> **5 cloves garlic**
> **$^1/_4$ teaspoon freshly ground black pepper**
> **1 tablespoon capers**
> **3 anchovy fillets, or 1 tablespoon anchovy paste**

FOR THE HORSERADISH SAUCE:

> **3 tablespoons extra-hot, cream-style horseradish**
> **$^1/_3$ cup sour cream**

1. To prepare the short ribs, in a small bowl combine the salt and pepper, and rub the mixture all over the ribs. Heat the olive oil in a large skillet over medium-high heat. Divide the ribs into 2 batches, and brown each batch on all sides until brown and crusty, about 3 to 4 minutes per side. Place the browned ribs in a large, heavy-bottomed pot or Dutch oven.

2. Add the carrots, celery, onions, balsamic vinegar, wine, broth, bouillon cube, rosemary, thyme, marjoram, bay leaves, garlic, and brown sugar to the pot. Cook over medium heat, covered, until the liquid starts to simmer, then lower the heat to medium-low and simmer, uncovered, for 3 hours, until the ribs are very tender and the braising liquid is reduced by about half.

3. Discard the bay leaves and the rosemary sprig.

4. To prepare the salsa verde, combine all ingredients in a food processor and process until smooth.

5. To prepare the horseradish sauce, in a small bowl combine the horseradish and the sour cream.

6. To serve, top the short ribs with a dollop of salsa verde and horseradish cream. Serve the braised short ribs with polenta or mashed potatoes.

Meat, Poultry & Seafood Dishes

MENU

Dinner with the In-Laws

Roasted Tomato Soup with Rosemary Croutons, page 35

Red Wine and Mushroom Risotto, page 96

Marionberry Tart with Honeyed Crème Fraîche, page 212

Happily Ever After
DESSERTS & SWEETS

Samoa Blondies

Chocolate Mudslide Cookies

Frozen Chocolate-Dipped Key Lime Pie Pops

Triple Chocolate Fudge Brownies

Nutella Doughnuts

Red Velvet Cake with Bourbon Cream Cheese Frosting

Pumpkin Brioche Bread Pudding with Warm Maple Cream

Lemon Sour Cream Pound Cake

Candy Bar Cupcakes

Dad's Favorite Carrot Cake with Whiskey Praline Cream Filling

Strawberry Rhubarb Pie

Marionberry Tart with Honeyed Crème Fraîche

Salted Caramel Pecan Tart

"MY HUSBAND COMES HOME EVERY NIGHT AND
SAYS, 'HOW CAN I HELP?': THE FOUR SWEETEST
WORDS IN THE ENGLISH LANGUAGE."

—*Janet Fletcher, author of* Fresh from the Farmers' Market *and*
Cheese & Wine: A Guide to Selecting, Pairing, and Enjoying

SAMOA BLONDIES

Makes about 16 squares

These addictive, slightly gooey, coconutty blondies are packed with chocolate chips and brown sugar, a combination inspired by the Samoa Girl Scout cookies adored by many. These simple, one-bowl sweets are easy to make and even more satisfying than the ones in boxes.

10 tablespoons unsalted butter
1 cup packed dark brown sugar
¼ cup granulated sugar
1 large egg
2 teaspoons vanilla extract
¼ teaspoon kosher salt
1¼ cups flour
1¼ cups sweetened flaked coconut
1¼ cups bittersweet or semisweet chocolate chips

1. Preheat the oven to 350°F. Grease an 8-by-8-inch baking pan and line the bottom with parchment paper.

2. Heat the butter in a small saucepan over high heat until it browns and smells nutty (keep an eye on it so it doesn't burn). Let the butter cool for a few moments, until just barely warm.

3. In a large mixing bowl, combine the browned butter and sugars. With a wooden spoon, mix in the egg, vanilla, and salt. Gradually stir in the flour, coconut, and chocolate chips until blended.

4. Pour the batter into the prepared pan and smooth the top with a rubber spatula. Bake for 25 to 30 minutes. (The center should still be soft—I like to pull them out at 25 minutes for a slightly gooey, underbaked blondie. Leaving them in for the full 30 minutes will ensure a completely baked blondie.) Let the blondie cool before turning it out onto a cutting board and slicing into squares.

Desserts & Sweets

CHOCOLATE MUDSLIDE COOKIES

Makes about 24 cookies

A fair warning: This cookie dough is so good, you might not end up with much batter to bake into cookies! Even if neither of you are unabashed cookie dough–lovin' people, you'll love this recipe for the ultra dark, intense chocolate cookies it yields. So be forewarned and have a glass of milk ready.

> **8 ounces bittersweet chocolate (preferably a premium brand, such as Valrhona), chopped**
> **³/₄ cup sugar**
> **3 tablespoons unsalted butter**
> **¹/₄ cup flour**
> **2 tablespoons cocoa powder**
> **¹/₄ teaspoon kosher salt**
> **¹/₂ teaspoon baking powder**
> **2 large eggs**
> **1 teaspoon vanilla extract**
> **1¹/₂ cups walnuts, roughly chopped**
> **6 ounces semisweet chocolate chips**

1. Preheat the oven to 350°F.

2. In a microwave-safe bowl, melt the chopped chocolate with the sugar and butter. Microwave in 20-second intervals, until about 80 percent of the chocolate has melted. Stir the chocolate mixture—the remaining chocolate will melt from the residual heat. Let cool to room temperature.

3. In a small bowl, combine the flour, cocoa powder, salt, and baking powder. Stir to combine.

4. In a large bowl, lightly beat the eggs with the vanilla. Slowly pour the microwaved chocolate mixture into the eggs in three additions, stirring between each addition. Stir the flour mixture into the chocolate batter until combined, then stir in the walnuts and chocolate chips.

5. On two light-colored baking sheets lined with parchment paper, drop heaping table-spoons of the cookie dough, leaving room for the cookies to spread (about 8 cookies per baking sheet). Use only the upper or middle oven rack for these cookies, as they have a tendency to burn on the lower rack.

6. Bake the cookies for 12 minutes. They will be slightly soft when they come out of the oven but will firm up as they cool.

Tiers of Joy

❧

THIERRY RAUTUREAU, CHEF-OWNER OF ROVER'S
IN SEATTLE, WASHINGTON, AND HIS WIFE, KATHY

Married: August 9, 1986

O ne would think that marrying a renowned French chef would be cause for intimidation in the kitchen. But Kathy Rautureau cooks almost seven nights a week for her family, which includes two teenagers and—when he's not cooking at his restaurant, Rover's—her husband, Thierry "The Chef in the Hat" Rautureau.

"I admit we don't cook together too often," Thierry says, "because I have a hard time holding back. But she's a great cook. She makes the best roast chicken I've ever had, anywhere. I fall in love with her whenever I eat it."

Food has always played a romantic role in the couple's relationship. They met while working at a Los Angeles restaurant where he was the chef and she was a waitress. After moving in together, Thierry did most of the cooking, always trying to find ways to woo his beautiful girlfriend through his artful French dishes.

At one point Kathy mentioned how much she loved *croquembouche*, an elaborate, cone-shaped French dessert of tiered pastries bound in a caramel cage, and Thierry secretly decided to make one for her in their tiny California kitchen.

"Making *croquembouche* is a long, long process. There are hours of work just to make the dough for the choux, let alone building the cone," Thierry explains, describing the laborious series of steps, delicate assemblage, and mountains of pans and equipment required. "It's not typically something you make for one person, but she was worth it."

Fortunately, Thierry's *croquembouche* had the desired effect ("I scored big points with that one," he laughs), although he admits it's not something he has considered duplicating again at home.

Now the couple lives in Seattle and eats simple meals inspired by the limitless fresh foods available in the Northwest.

"As I grow older and time becomes more important, I really like being in the kitchen with Kathy and the kids," Thierry says. "I get in the way sometimes—I like to put my grain of salt everywhere—but I have a lot of appreciation for anyone who cooks for me. It's a beautiful thing, when you think about it."

ADVICE FOR NEWLYWEDS: *"Make a tighter shopping list. People are usually afraid to cook with leftovers, so make sure you are buying what you need."*

—Thierry

FAVORITE THINGS IN THE KITCHEN: *"A good-old Weber grill in the backyard and stainless steel heavy pots and pans."*

—Thierry

FROZEN CHOCOLATE-DIPPED KEY LIME PIE POPS

Makes 8 pie pops

There's a company called Kermit's Key West Key Lime Shoppe that makes and ships frozen chocolate-covered key lime pie pops. When I read about this mind-numbingly delicious concoction on the Internet, my eyes bugged out of my head, and I knew I had to come up with a recipe for them so that I'd have a steady supply in my freezer. If you don't want to go through the hassle of inserting the popsicle sticks in each treat, you can just slice and serve the frozen key lime pie as is or with a drizzle of chocolate.

FOR THE CRUST:

1¼ cups graham cracker crumbs

6 tablespoons unsalted butter, melted

2 tablespoons sugar

Pinch of kosher salt

FOR THE FILLING:

One 14-ounce can sweetened condensed milk

3 teaspoons (about 3 key limes) freshly grated key lime zest

⅔ cup (about 1½ pounds key limes) freshly squeezed key lime juice

4 egg yolks

FOR THE CHOCOLATE DIPPING SAUCE:

6 ounces bittersweet chocolate, chopped

½ cup heavy cream

1 tablespoon unsalted butter

OPTIONAL GARNISHES:

Toasted coconut

Chopped, toasted macadamia nuts

1. Preheat the oven to 350°F.

2. To make the crust, process the graham cracker crumbs in a food processor until they're pulverized. (If you don't have a food processor, place the graham crackers in a resealable plastic bag and bash them with a rolling pin until they turn to rubble.)

3. Put the graham cracker crumbs in a large bowl and add the melted butter, sugar, and salt. Press the crumbs into an 8-inch aluminum pie plate, spreading them evenly over the bottom and up the sides.

4. To make the filling, in a medium bowl whisk together the condensed milk, key lime zest and juice, and egg yolks. Pour the filling into the crust. (If the filling does not quite reach the top of the crust, gently press the crust down with a spoon until it is level with the filling. This is to ensure a neat, smooth key lime popsicle.)

5. Bake the pie for 10 minutes.

6. To make the popsicles, remove the pie from the oven, cover tightly with plastic wrap, and place in the freezer for 45 minutes.

7. Score the surface of the pie lightly to divide it into 8 wedges. On the outside of your foil pan, cut a popsicle stick–size slit in the center of what will be the base of your popsicles. Carefully insert a popsicle stick in each slit, centering it as best you can. Cover the pie and return it to the freezer for at least 4 hours (or overnight).

8. With scissors, snip the aluminum pie plate away from the frozen pie. Cut the pie into 8 wedges, using the lines you scored as a guide.

9. To make the chocolate dipping sauce, in a microwave-safe bowl, melt the chocolate with the heavy cream. Microwave in 20-second intervals, until about 80 percent of the chocolate has melted. Stir the chocolate mixture—the remaining chocolate will melt from the residual heat. Stir in the butter.

10. Dip each popsicle in chocolate and place them on a parchment- or Silpat-lined baking tray. Sprinkle with the toasted coconut and chopped macadamia nuts. Place the popsicles back in the freezer for at least 1 hour so the chocolate can harden before serving. The popsicles will keep, well-wrapped, in the freezer for up to 2 weeks.

Desserts & Sweets

TRIPLE CHOCOLATE FUDGE BROWNIES

Makes 24 brownies

These super-dark, fudgy brownies are a dream dessert: the perfect amalgamation of three kinds of chocolate, cocoa powder, and a smattering of espresso powder to further enhance that deep chocolate flavor. This recipe has been in the making for eight years and contains over a pound of the good stuff. Have leftovers? Freeze individually wrapped brownies so you can sneak one into both you and your love's lunch bags every day of the week.

> 8 ounces unsweetened chocolate, coarsely chopped
> 6 ounces bittersweet chocolate, coarsely chopped
> 1 cup (2 sticks) unsalted butter
> 1³/₄ cups sugar
> 2 tablespoons cocoa powder
> 5 large eggs
> 1 tablespoon vanilla extract
> ³/₄ teaspoon espresso powder
> ¹/₂ teaspoon kosher salt
> 1 cup flour
> 6 ounces chocolate chips (semisweet, bittersweet, or white—
>   pick your favorite)
> 1¹/₂ cups chopped walnuts, pecans, or hazelnuts (optional)

1. Preheat the oven to 325°F.

2. Grease a 13-by-9-inch glass or light-colored rectangular pan and line the bottom with parchment paper.

3. In a microwave-safe bowl, melt the unsweetened chocolate and bittersweet chocolate with the butter. Microwave in 20-second intervals, until about 80 percent of the chocolate has melted. Stir the chocolate mixture—the remaining chocolate will melt from the residual heat. Set aside to cool.

4. In a large bowl, stir together the sugar, cocoa powder, eggs, vanilla, espresso powder, and salt. Add the cooled chocolate mixture and stir until combined. Stir in the flour, chocolate chips, and the nuts.

5. Pour the brownie batter into the prepared pan and bake for 30 to 35 minutes. Don't overbake the brownies—they should be slightly soft in the center when you remove them from the oven. For cleaner slices, wrap the brownies in plastic wrap and freeze for 1 hour before slicing. The brownies will keep, well wrapped, in the freezer for up to 2 weeks.

NUTELLA DOUGHNUTS

Makes about 14 doughnuts

Think doughnuts are hard to make at home? Think again! Try this recipe when you're both craving a sweet postdinner treat. Simply make the batter for these fluffy, tender ricotta doughnuts, fry them up, and fill them with Nutella, a popular Italian chocolate-hazelnut spread. Use the same recipe, adding 1½ teaspoons grated lemon or orange zest to the dough, to make jelly- or lemon curd–filled doughnuts.

> **3 large eggs**
> **¼ cup sugar**
> **8 ounces whole-milk ricotta**
> **½ teaspoon kosher salt**
> **1 teaspoon vanilla extract**
> **1 cup flour**
> **2 teaspoons baking powder**
> **Canola, vegetable, or peanut oil for frying**
> **Powdered sugar for dusting doughnuts**
> **1 cup Nutella**

1. In a large mixing bowl, stir together the eggs, sugar, ricotta, salt, and vanilla extract. Add the flour and baking powder, and mix until just combined.

2. Heat 3 inches of the oil in a deep pot until it registers 365°F on a deep-fat thermometer. Drop a tablespoon of batter into the oil and cook for about 3 minutes on one side, and 2 to 3 minutes on the other side. (Do not make the doughnuts much bigger, as the outside will brown too quickly and they won't cook through.) Don't overcrowd the pot—you will probably need to fry the doughnuts in three batches. Cut one doughnut open to make sure it's cooked through before removing the rest of the batch from the oil. When the doughnuts are cooked, scoop them out and allow them to drain on paper towels. Repeat with remaining batter.

3. Dust the doughnuts with powdered sugar and pipe Nutella into the center of each one using a piping bag outfitted with a medium pastry tip (I use a 4 millimeter 30-5 Kaiser tip). Insert the tip into the center of each doughnut and gently squeeze in the filling. These doughnuts are meant to be devoured warm out of the fryer, so make them just before you're both ready to eat them.

RED VELVET CAKE WITH BOURBON CREAM CHEESE FROSTING

Makes one 3-layer cake, serves 12 to 14

This towering, crimson-hued cake, sandwiched between thick, billowy clouds of bourbon cream cheese frosting, is a sight that draws a smile from the most vehement dessert hater. Red velvet cake is a Southern classic, flavored with a bit of cocoa powder and tangy buttermilk. This recipe was perfected over many years, and it's the perfect way to indulge on each other's birthdays. Best of all, this is a dump-and-mix recipe, meaning that all the cake ingredients are basically just stirred together in one bowl. No creaming butter! No fussy, drawn-out instructions! This is one cake you'll both make over and over again.

> 3 cups flour
> $2^{1}/_{4}$ cups sugar
> $1^{1}/_{4}$ teaspoons baking soda
> $1^{1}/_{4}$ teaspoons kosher salt
> $^{1}/_{4}$ cup cocoa powder
> $1^{1}/_{4}$ cups buttermilk
> 4 large eggs, beaten
> 2 tablespoons vanilla extract
> $1^{1}/_{2}$ tablespoons white vinegar
> 2 cups neutral oil, such as vegetable, peanut, or canola
> 1-ounce bottle red food coloring, or $^{1}/_{2}$ tube gel food coloring
> Bourbon Cream Cheese Frosting (recipe follows)

1. Preheat the oven to 300°F.

2. Grease three 9-inch round cake pans and line the bottoms with parchment paper.

3. In a large bowl, stir together the flour, sugar, baking soda, salt, and cocoa powder. Make a well in the center of the dry ingredients, and stir in the buttermilk, eggs, vanilla, vinegar, oil, and food coloring. Divide the batter evenly into the cake pans.

Desserts & Sweets

RED VELVET CAKE WITH BOURBON
CREAM CHEESE FROSTING

4. Bake the cakes for 30 to 40 minutes, or until a toothpick inserted in the center comes out clean. While the cakes are still hot, wrap them in plastic wrap to "steam" them slightly. (This extra step makes the cakes moister.) Unwrap the cakes when they cool to room temperature.

5. Place one cake layer on a serving platter and spoon ¾ cup of the Bourbon Cream Cheese Frosting over the top. Spread evenly and then stack the next cake layer on top. Repeat the frosting and stacking with the remaining cake layer. Smooth a very thin layer of frosting all over the sides of the cakes to set crumbs and coat the cake edges. Finally, coat the sides and top of the cake with one more thin layer of frosting. Serve immediately. (Leftover cake can be covered and stored in the refrigerator for up to 3 days.)

BOURBON CREAM CHEESE FROSTING

Makes 5 cups of frosting

> 1¼ cups (2½ sticks) unsalted butter, softened
> Three 8-ounce packages cream cheese, softened
> 2 cups icing sugar, sifted
> 2½ tablespoons bourbon
> 1 tablespoon vanilla extract

1. In a large bowl, with an electric mixer on medium speed, beat the butter and cream cheese until smooth. Turn the mixer down to low and add the icing sugar gradually, beating until light and smooth. Add the bourbon and vanilla extract, and beat again until smooth.

PUMPKIN BRIOCHE BREAD PUDDING WITH WARM MAPLE CREAM

Serves 8 to 10

The reason this bread pudding is so custardy is because it's double-soaked with a lovely base scented with cinnamon, nutmeg, and cloves. When the pale orange–hued pudding emerges from the oven, a few lashings of warm, spiced maple cream send it over the edge. For a holiday dessert none of your relatives will forget, pair this pudding with ginger or maple walnut ice cream.

You'll need to start this recipe the night before you plan on serving it.

2 loaves brioche, thinly sliced

$^3/_4$ cup (1$^1/_2$ sticks) unsalted butter, softened

2 tablespoons ground cinnamon

2 teaspoons ground nutmeg

1 teaspoon ground cloves

1 teaspoon kosher salt

5 large eggs

4 egg yolks

3$^1/_2$ cups heavy cream

3 cups whole milk

1$^1/_2$ cups light brown sugar

2 tablespoons vanilla extract

One 29-ounce can pumpkin purée

Maple Cream (recipe follows)

1. Grease a large ovenproof baking dish. Spread the brioche slices with the butter, then stack them and slice on the diagonal to make triangles. Lay the brioche triangles in the prepared dish, overlapping them.

2. In a large bowl whisk together the cinnamon, nutmeg, cloves, salt, eggs, egg yolks, cream, milk, brown sugar, vanilla, and pumpkin purée. Pour three quarters of the mixture over the brioche. Cover the remaining custard base and refrigerate. Then cover the brioche and refrigerate overnight, so it has plenty of time to absorb the custard.

3. Remove the brioche from the refrigerator and poke holes all over the surface using a fork. Pour the remaining custard over the brioche and let it sit at room temperature for about 2 hours, until it absorbs all the custard.

4. Preheat the oven to 350°F.

5. Bake the bread pudding for about 1 hour, or until it puffs slightly and is just barely set. Serve warm, with the Maple Cream poured on top.

MAPLE CREAM

Makes 3½ cups

>   **4 cups heavy cream**
>   **½ teaspoon kosher salt**
>   **1 tablespoon ground cinnamon**
>   **1 teaspoon ground nutmeg**
>   **One 12-ounce bottle Grade B maple syrup**
>   **⅓ cup sugar**

1. To make the maple cream, combine all the ingredients in a large saucepan and cook over medium heat, stirring occasionally, for 30 to 40 minutes, or until reduced and thickened. Taste for seasoning, adding another small pinch or two of salt if you prefer a salty-sweet flavor combination.

Make Your Cake and Eat It Too

⠂⢾❧⠂

JANET FLETCHER, FOOD WRITER AND AUTHOR OF
FRESH FROM THE FARMERS' MARKET AND DOUGLAS
FLETCHER, VICE PRESIDENT OF WINEMAKING FOR
THE TERLATO WINE GROUP

Married: April 29, 1984

Some desserts are so precious they needn't appear more than every quarter century. When Douglas and Janet Fletcher married in a DIY wedding in Berkeley, California, in 1984, they not only arranged bouquets from market flowers and said their vows in a friend's backyard, but chose to make their own wedding cake: a three-layer, spiced pecan cake coated in buttercream icing. The recipe, featured in *Bon Appétit* magazine, was by famed chef Paul Prudhomme, but the couple gave the confection their own signature spin by first brushing each layer with Jamaican rum–flavored simple syrup. "We were excited to create this project together," says Janet, an award-winning food writer and cookbook author. "But after it was done, we looked at each other and said, 'Never again!'"

The wedding cake was a huge hit; in fact, Janet and Douglas never got a taste, beyond the requisite ceremonial first bites. The entire cake vanished into their guests' bellies within minutes.

Later that day, one of Douglas's colleagues in the wine industry approached the couple, begging them to make the same cake for his wedding later that summer.

"Suddenly, we were in the wedding cake business," Janet laughs. "The second cake came out even better than the first. But now we really meant it: never again!" This time, when another couple inevitably implored them to re-create the now-famous cake for *their* upcoming nuptials, the Fletchers declined.

Prudhomme's spiced pecan cake spent the next twenty-five years living only in the Fletchers' memories and the pages of an old, weathered *Bon Appétit* until the couple began planning their silver wedding anniversary.

The couple decided to revisit the recipe they'd never had a chance to enjoy the first time around.

This time they made a single layer cake brushed with their signature Jamaican rum simple syrup and skipped the buttercream.

"It was more of a ceremonial nod to our wedding cake rather than an authentic re-creation," Janet says. "But it was still fun to walk down memory lane."

Janet and Douglas live full-time in Napa, California, and cook together every night, creating meals from their expansive garden or from the recipes Janet is testing for the various publications she writes for.

"It's how we connect every day," Janet says. "Sharing a love of food and wine has been an important element of our marriage's success. It's a glue that keeps us together."

ADVICE FOR NEWLYWEDS: *"Start small with simple things you both like that won't create a sink full of dishes, such as risotto, frittata, or an omelet. Once you've mastered that, you can make variations and introduce the flavors you like."*

—Janet

FAVORITE THINGS IN THE KITCHEN: *"A collection of mortars and pestles in different sizes and materials we've gathered from around the world."*

—Janet

LEMON SOUR CREAM POUND CAKE

Serves 12 to 14

I get my love of baking from my mother, a most extraordinary woman, who made puff pastry from scratch in the early '80s, with no Food Network, food blogs, or cooking magazines to guide her. My mother especially loves lemon pound cake with a moist crumb and a tangy drizzle of citrus frosting—I created this recipe especially for her. Invite your own mothers over to sample a slice. This recipe makes two cake loaves (or one large bundt cake), and you'll need a total of about seven lemons for the full recipe. Be sure to zest three or four of the lemons before you juice them—you'll need the zest for the cake batter as well as for the glaze.

FOR THE POUND CAKE:

3 cups cake flour

$^1/_2$ teaspoon baking soda

$^1/_2$ teaspoon baking powder

$^3/_4$ teaspoon kosher salt

1 cup (2 sticks) unsalted butter

2 cups sugar

6 large eggs

$^1/_4$ cup (about 2 lemons) freshly squeezed lemon juice

2 tablespoons (about 2 lemons) freshly grated lemon zest

1 teaspoon vanilla extract

1 teaspoon lemon extract

$^3/_4$ cup sour cream

FOR THE LEMON SYRUP:

$^1/_3$ cup (about 3 lemons) freshly squeezed lemon juice

$^1/_3$ cup sugar

3 tablespoons water

FOR THE LEMON SOUR CREAM GLAZE:

$^1/_4$ cup sour cream

$2^1/_2$ cups icing sugar, sifted

3 tablespoons (about $1^1/_2$ lemons) freshly squeezed lemon juice

1 tablespoon (about 1 lemon) freshly grated lemon zest

1. To make the cake, preheat the oven to 325°F.

2. Grease a standard tube pan or two loaf pans. (Cut a piece of greased parchment to fit the bottom of the pan for extra insurance, if you'd like.)

3. Sift the flour, baking soda, baking powder, and salt together in a large mixing bowl.

4. In another large bowl, cream the butter with an electric mixer on medium speed until pale and fluffy, about 3 to 4 minutes. Gradually add the sugar and beat for another 2 minutes. Add the eggs one by one, mixing well after each addition. Beat in the lemon juice and zest, and the vanilla and lemon extracts. Turn off the mixer and scrape down the sides of the bowl. Using a rubber spatula, mix in half the dry ingredients, then the sour cream. Mix in the remaining dry ingredients until just combined (overmixing will cause the cake to be tough).

5. Transfer the batter to the prepared pan.

6. For a large pound cake, bake for 1 hour and 30 minutes, or until a toothpick inserted in the middle of the cake comes out clean. For two loaf cakes, bake for 1 hour to 1 hour and 10 minutes, or until a toothpick inserted in the middle of the cakes comes out clean.

7. Set the cake aside to cool while you make the lemon syrup and lemon sour cream glaze.

8. To make the lemon syrup, combine all the ingredients together in a small saucepan and bring to a simmer over low heat, letting the mixture reduce for a few minutes until thick and syrupy. Let cool.

9. To make the lemon sour cream glaze, whisk all the ingredients together in a medium bowl.

10. To assemble the cake, when it is cool, run a knife along the edge and invert it onto a serving plate. With a wooden skewer or toothpick, poke holes all over the top of the cake. Carefully spoon the lemon syrup over the cake, letting the syrup absorb before spooning more over the top.

11. When the cake has absorbed the syrup, drizzle the glaze over the top.

CANDY BAR CUPCAKES

Makes 20 to 22 cupcakes

These cupcakes are a grown-up take on a childhood treat. A piece of Snickers candy bar is nestled inside each moist, chocolaty cake, which is then topped with salted caramel–peanut butter frosting. The frosting is also wonderful sandwiched between Chocolate Mudslide Cookies (page 184).

FOR THE CUPCAKES:

4 Snickers bars, cut into ½-inch pieces

3 ounces good-quality bittersweet chocolate, such as Valrhona 70 percent, finely chopped

1 cup strong, hot brewed coffee

2 large eggs

²/₃ cup vegetable oil

1 cup buttermilk

1 teaspoon vanilla

2 cups sugar

2 cups flour

1 cup good-quality unsweetened cocoa powder

2 teaspoons baking powder

1 teaspoon kosher salt

FOR THE FROSTING:

¹/₃ cup heavy cream

¹/₃ cup granulated sugar

3 tablespoons water

³/₄ cup (1½ sticks) unsalted butter, softened

²/₃ cup creamy peanut butter

1 teaspoon vanilla extract

1 teaspoon kosher salt

³/₄ cup powdered sugar

Chopped, honey-roasted peanuts, for garnish (optional)

Desserts & Sweets

CANDY BAR
CUPCAKES

1. Freeze the Snickers bar pieces for at least 2 hours, until hardened.

2. Preheat the oven to 350°F. In a small bowl, mix together the chocolate and the hot coffee until the chocolate dissolves. Set aside until the coffee mixture cools.

3. In a separate large bowl, with an electric mixer on medium-high speed, beat the eggs for 4 to 5 minutes, until pale in color and almost doubled in volume. Reduce mixer speed to medium and add the vegetable oil, buttermilk, and vanilla, and beat until combined. Add the coffee and chocolate mixture, and again beat until combined.

4. Add the sugar, flour, cocoa powder, baking powder, and salt, and mix just until the batter comes together and no white streaks of flour are visible. Take care not to over-mix, as this will make your cupcakes tough.

5. Divide the batter into lined cupcake tins, filling them three quarters full. Place a frozen Snickers piece in the center of each cupcake. Bake for 20 to 25 minutes, until the tops of the cupcakes spring back when lightly pressed (or a toothpick inserted in the center of one of the cupcakes comes out clean).

6. Let the cupcakes cool on a wire rack before frosting.

7. To make the frosting, first make sure you have your heavy cream measured out and close at hand. Combine the sugar and water in a small saucepan over high heat. The sugar will begin to liquefy and turn brown around the edges—using a heatproof spatula, drag the brown bits toward the center, so the caramel doesn't get too dark in some areas. Once the caramel has turned a deep amber brown, 7 to 8 minutes, immediately turn the heat off and pour the cream in. (The caramel will bubble up, then quickly subside—don't be scared!) Stir the caramel, then allow it to cool to room temperature before proceeding.

8. In a medium bowl, add the butter, peanut butter, vanilla, and salt. Using an electric mixer on medium speed, beat until combined, then reduce to medium-low and add the powdered sugar. Beat until the frosting becomes light and fluffy, about 3 to 4 minutes. Pour in the cooled caramel and continue to beat until combined. Store the frosting in the refrigerator until ready to use.

9. Spread each cooled cupcake with a heaping tablespoon of frosting, then garnish with a sprinkle of peanuts, if desired.

DAD'S FAVORITE CARROT CAKE WITH WHISKEY PRALINE CREAM FILLING

Serves 10 to 12

One of my fondest memories in high school was sharing coffee and carrot cake with my dad in the afternoon—oh, how grown-up I felt! I created this recipe especially for him. Try it out on your dads (or anyone with a weakness for carroty and cream cheesy sweetness). Recently, I've taken to adding a whiskey praline cream layer to this classic cake, and I've also included some orange zest and orange liqueur in the frosting to take it from coffeehouse favorite to retro-luxe sophistication!

FOR THE CARROT CAKE:

2 cups flour

3 teaspoons ground cinnamon

1 teaspoon ground nutmeg

2 teaspoons baking powder

1 teaspoon kosher salt

1 cup (2 sticks) unsalted butter, softened

1¾ cups sugar

4 large eggs

¼ cup vegetable oil

3 cups (6 to 7 medium) carrots, grated

1 cup chopped walnuts

One 8-ounce can crushed pineapple, drained well

½ cup sweetened flaked coconut

1½ cups chopped, toasted walnuts, for garnish (optional)

FOR THE WHISKEY PRALINE CREAM FILLING:

¼ cup heavy cream

3 tablespoons unsalted butter

⅓ cup sugar

3 tablespoons water

½ cup chopped walnuts

Pinch of kosher salt

1 tablespoon whiskey

FOR THE ORANGE CREAM CHEESE FROSTING:

1 cup (2 sticks) unsalted butter
Two 8-ounce packages cream cheese, softened
2½ cups icing sugar, sifted
1 tablespoon orange liqueur, such as Grand Marnier (or substitute
2 tablespoons freshly squeezed orange juice)
Zest of 1 medium orange (about 2 tablespoons)

1. To make the cake, preheat the oven to 350°F. Grease two 9-inch round baking pans and line the bottoms with parchment paper.

2. In a medium bowl, whisk together the flour, cinnamon, nutmeg, baking powder, and salt until just combined.

3. In a large bowl, with an electric mixer on medium speed, beat the butter and sugar together until light and fluffy, about 4 minutes. Add the eggs and oil, and beat until just combined. With a wooden spoon, stir in the carrots, walnuts, pineapple, and coconut until thoroughly mixed. Add the flour mixture and stir again until combined.

4. Divide the batter into the prepared pans. Smooth the top of the batter with a rubber spatula and bake for 35 to 40 minutes, or until a toothpick inserted in the middle of the cakes comes out clean.

5. Run a knife along the edge of the cakes to loosen them from the pans and turn them out onto a cooling rack. Let cool completely before frosting.

6. To make the filling, first make sure you have the cream and butter measured out and close at hand. Combine the sugar and water in a small saucepan over high heat. The sugar will begin to liquefy and turn brown around the edges—using a heatproof spatula, drag the brown bits toward the center, so the caramel doesn't get too dark in some areas. Once the caramel has turned a deep amber brown, 7 to 8 minutes, immediately turn the heat off and pour the cream in. (The caramel will bubble up, then quickly subside—don't be scared!) Add the butter, and stir until it melts. Lower the heat to medium-low and cook the caramel so it reduces and thickens slightly, about 2 minutes. Add the walnuts, salt, and whiskey, and take the pan off the heat to cool.

7. To make the frosting, in a large bowl, with an electric mixer on medium speed, beat the butter and cream cheese together until smooth. Add the icing sugar, orange liqueur, and orange zest. Beat until the frosting becomes light and fluffy, 5 to 6 minutes.

8. To assemble the cake, place one layer on a cake stand and spread the whiskey praline frosting evenly over the surface. Top with the second layer and frost the entire cake with the cream cheese frosting. Press the walnut pieces on the sides of the cake, if desired.

Desserts & Sweets

STRAWBERRY RHUBARB PIE

Serves 8

Is there any dessert more evocative of early summer than strawberry rhubarb pie? Surprise your sweetheart after dinner with a warm slice, topped with a big, melting scoop of vanilla ice cream.

You will have extra pie scraps from the crust recipe. I like to sprinkle the scraps with cinnamon sugar and bake them for 30 minutes at 350°F (you can do this at the same time you're baking the pie)—a sweet treat for the cook!

FOR THE CRUST:

3 cups flour

1^1/$_2$ tablespoons sugar, plus additional for sprinkling

1 teaspoon kosher salt

^{1}/$_4$ teaspoon baking powder

^{3}/$_4$ cup cold leaf lard*

^{1}/$_2$ cup (1 stick) cold unsalted butter

One 8-ounce container sour cream

1 egg yolk

2 tablespoons whole milk

FOR THE FILLING:

3 cups sliced strawberries

4 cups sliced rhubarb, divided

1 cup sugar

1^1/$_2$ teaspoons ground cinnamon

^{1}/$_2$ teaspoon ground nutmeg

^{1}/$_4$ teaspoon kosher salt

Zest of 1 large lemon (about 1 tablespoon)

^{1}/$_4$ cup cornstarch or tapioca starch

3 tablespoons water

---

* *Leaf lard is the highest grade of lard; it is available at many farmers markets, or you can substitute an equal amount of regular lard, shortening, or butter.*

1. To make the crust, in a large mixing bowl combine the flour, sugar, salt, and baking powder. With a pastry cutter or two knives, cut the leaf lard and the butter into the flour until pea-size chunks form. Mix in the sour cream, then gather the dough together. On a lightly floured surface, knead once or twice. (If the dough seems too wet and sticky to knead, add a tablespoon of flour. Don't knead more than a few times—you still want to see the specks of butter in the dough, which is what will give you a flaky crust.) Divide the dough in half, and form each half into a ball. Flatten each ball to create two discs, then wrap them in plastic wrap. Refrigerate the dough for at least 1 hour (or up to overnight) before proceeding.

2. While the dough is chilling, make the filling. In a large saucepan, combine the strawberries, rhubarb, sugar, cinnamon, nutmeg, salt, and lemon zest. Bring to a simmer over medium heat and cook, stirring, for 3 to 4 minutes, until the fruit gets juicy and soft.

3. In a small bowl, dissolve the cornstarch in the water. Stir the cornstarch slurry into the filling and cook until the mixture bubbles and thickens, about 2 to 3 minutes. Let cool before filling the pie.

4. Preheat the oven to 425°F.

5. On a clean, floured surface, using a floured rolling pin, roll one disc of the dough into a circle about 12 inches in diameter and ⅛ inch thick. Gently roll up the dough using your rolling pin, then lay it over the pie plate and unroll so it falls inside. Gently press the dough down so it lines the bottom and sides of the pie plate. Trim the excess dough to leave a ½-inch overhang.

6. Add the filling, then roll out the second piece of dough in the same fashion and lay it on top of the pie. Pinch the top and bottom pieces of dough together to form an edge, then trim the top piece of dough, leaving about a ½-inch overhang. Crimp the edges together with a fork dipped in flour, or flute the edges together by pinching the dough between your thumb and forefinger. With a knife, cut a few steam vents in the top of the pie.

7. In a small bowl, whisk together the egg yolk and milk. Lightly brush the crust with a bit of the beaten egg yolk mixture and sprinkle with a little sugar, if desired.

8. Bake the pie at 425°F for 20 minutes. Check the crust: if it is browning too fast, cover the edge with a pie shield. Lower the temperature to 350°F and bake for another 30 to 35 minutes, or until the crust is completely brown and crisp.

Love Is Apple Pie

KATE McDERMOTT, PIE GURU, AND JON ROWLEY,
FOOD CONSULTANT AND TASTEMAKER

Married: July 28, 2001

Most wedding registries don't make a story in the pages of *The New Yorker*, but then again, most weddings aren't like that of Kate McDermott and Jon Rowley. The couple met on GardenWeb .com and, once engaged, invited their foodie friends to send garden mulch—that's right: biodegradable *garbage*—in lieu of gifts. Food luminaries such as Ruth Reichl, Julia Child, Jeffrey Steingarten, and Sheila Lukins gift-wrapped banana peels, coffee grounds, old cake, and spent hops for the "wedding compost," which Kate and Jon planned to use for mulching a commemorative wedding rosebush.

"It was spectacular," Jon laughs. "You've never seen better-looking mulch."

Now married, the couple gets great pleasure from their frequent "food adventures." Weekends might find them foraging for mushrooms near Mount Rainier; road-tripping to the coast to nab the season's first anchovies, mussels, or oysters; or perfecting the Apple Pie Project, their four-year quest to create the quintessential American apple pie.

"I've always had an idea about what the perfect apple pie should be," Jon says, "and Kate is a wonderful baker. We found this project to be a serious collaboration and very enjoyable."

The couple couldn't have guessed the depth and length the project would command when they set out, but Jon has spent a professional lifetime sussing out the perfect flavors of foods, so naturally he put much thought into the pie. For the filling, years of testing revealed that only hard-to-find heirloom varieties, such as Gravensteins, Esopus Spitzenbergs, and Cox's Orange Pippins, with skins intact, held the correct concentration of sweetness. (Jon used a refractometer, a geekish gadget that tests sugar content, to determine the right varieties.)

Kate took over the crust research (Jon critiqued), and the pair baked and baked and baked. They took detailed notes on fruit color, shape, and texture; how the apple skin imparted depth of aroma and flavor when cooked; which flours and butters made the most tender, flaky crust; and so on. Over time, as their perfect pie took shape, Kate and Jon deeply bonded over their special project.

"In the end it's about the love that goes into the pie," Kate says. "People pick up on that and can taste it."

"Love *is* apple pie," Jon says. "What else could be more nurturing, more comforting, more wholesome?"

ADVICE FOR NEWLYWEDS: *"When baking, we are processing food with our hands and our hearts. Think about this process when you are cooking or baking. It is what makes some pies good and other pies soar."*

—*Kate*

FAVORITE THINGS IN THE KITCHEN: *"Pie pan."*

—*Kate*

"Black cast-iron skillet."

—*Jon*

MARIONBERRY TART WITH HONEYED CRÈME FRAÎCHE

Serves 8

This is a much-beloved recipe, ideal for any spring or summertime dinner party. The berries in the tart are nestled under a soft, golden-brown crust that bakes up slightly puffed and golden. The combination of sweet honey and tangy crème fraîche is a surprising yet wonderful accompaniment. If crème fraîche is not available, you can easily replace it with an equal amount of sour cream for the same delicious results. (Can't find marionberries? Any berry would be a great substitute.)

FOR THE CRUST:

2 tablespoons heavy cream

1 egg yolk, beaten

½ cup (1 stick) unsalted butter, cut into ¼-inch cubes

3 tablespoons sugar

1 cup plus 5 tablespoons flour

¼ teaspoon kosher salt

FOR THE FILLING:

3 cups fresh or frozen marionberries (or berries of your choice)

½ cup (1 stick) unsalted butter

2 large eggs

¾ cup sugar

½ teaspoon kosher salt

3 tablespoons flour

1 teaspoon vanilla extract

1 tablespoon rum or bourbon (optional)

Honeyed Crème Fraîche (recipe follows)

1. To make the crust, whisk the cream and egg yolk together in a small bowl. In a large bowl, with an electric mixer at medium speed, beat together the butter and sugar until creamy, about 2 to 3 minutes. Add the flour and salt and continue to beat until the dough just comes together. Reduce mixer speed to low, add the egg yolk mixture, and beat until just combined, taking care not to overmix.

MARIONBERRY TART
WITH HONEYED
CRÈME FRAÎCHE

2.   Wrap the dough in plastic wrap and pat it into a flat disc about 1 inch thick. Refrigerate for about 30 minutes before proceeding.

3.   After the dough has chilled, on a lightly floured surface roll it to a thickness of $1/4$ inch, then place it in a 9-inch tart pan with a removable bottom. Trim the edges so the dough is flush with the top of the pan. Cover with plastic wrap and refrigerate the crust for 30 minutes before proceeding.

4.   Preheat the oven to 375°F.

5.   Place a piece of parchment paper over the crust and fill the lined tart shell with pie weights or beans. Bake for 18 to 20 minutes, or until the crust turns lightly golden. Carefully remove the parchment paper and pie weights.

6.   Lower the oven temperature to 350°F.

7.   To make the filling, sprinkle the berries evenly over the bottom of the tart shell. In a small saucepan, melt the butter over medium heat until lightly browned, 3 to 4 minutes.

8.   In a medium bowl, with an electric mixer at medium speed, beat together the eggs and sugar until thick and creamy, about 3 to 5 minutes. Add the salt, flour, vanilla, and rum, and stir with a wooden spoon to combine. Stir in the browned butter. Pour the custard over the berries, then bake the tart for 40 to 45 minutes, or until the custard is lightly browned. Cool the tart in the pan before slicing. Serve each slice of tart with a dollop of Honeyed Crème Fraîche.

HONEYED CRÈME FRAÎCHE

Makes about $3/4$ cup

8 ounces crème fraîche or sour cream
$1/4$ cup honey

1.   Beat the crème fraîche with a wire whisk for 1 to 2 minutes, until it thickens slightly, then whisk in the honey.

SALTED CARAMEL PECAN TART

Serves 8 to 10

A bit of salt in something as sweet as caramel can be an addictive combination. This fusion of flavors—a buttery, sweet tart crust; salty caramel; and toasted pecans—will satisfy your sweet *and* salty cravings. I've baked this tart more times than I can count. Make it even better by serving it with a scoop of chocolate sorbet or a wisp of plain whipped cream on the side—just try not to eat it all in one sitting!

FOR THE CRUST:

1 recipe tart crust dough (see page 212)

FOR THE PECAN CARAMEL FILLING:

³/₄ cup heavy cream

4 tablespoons (¹/₂ stick) unsalted butter

2 cups sugar

³/₄ cup water

¹/₂ teaspoon kosher salt

2¹/₄ cups toasted pecans

1. To make the crust, line a 9-inch tart pan with the dough. Trim the edges so the dough is flush with the top of the pan. Chill the crust in the refrigerator for 30 minutes before proceeding.

2. Preheat the oven to 375°F.

3. Place a piece of parchment paper over the crust, and fill the lined tart shell with pie weights or beans. Bake for 20 minutes. Take the tart from the oven, and remove the pie weights and parchment paper. Return the tart to the oven and bake for another 10 minutes, or until the crust is golden brown.

4. To make the filling, first make sure you have your cream and butter measured out and close at hand. In a large, heavy-bottomed pot or Dutch oven, combine the sugar and water over high heat. The sugar will begin to liquefy and turn brown around the edges—using a heatproof spatula, drag the brown bits toward the center, so the caramel doesn't get too dark in some areas. Once the caramel has turned a deep amber color, 7 to 8 minutes, immediately turn the heat off and pour the cream in. (The caramel will bubble up, then quickly subside—don't be scared!) Add the butter, and stir until it

melts. Lower the heat to medium and cook, stirring, until the caramel thickens a bit, about 5 minutes. Add the salt and let the caramel cool a bit before taking a tiny taste to adjust the seasoning, adding a pinch more salt if you'd like. (Be careful, it's hot: blow on the spoon before tasting.)

5. Coarsely chop half of the pecans and leave the rest whole. (This gives a nicer texture to the filling.) Stir the pecans into the caramel. Fill the tart shell with the caramel and let the tart firm up in the refrigerator for at least 3 hours (or overnight) before slicing.

MENU

A Special Anniversary

Anniversary Pea Soup with Seared Sea Scallops, page 31

Braised Short Ribs with Salsa Verde and Horseradish Cream, page 178

Salted Caramel Pecan Tart, page 215

Acknowledgments

First, I would like to offer my sincere thanks to the entire team at Sasquatch Books—particularly Gary Luke, Tara Spicer, and Rachelle Longé—for believing in me and for being supportive and encouraging every step of the way. Thank you also to Diane Sepanski for her very precise copyedit. I would also like to thank Kathryn Barnard for shooting such gorgeous photos and her food stylist, Patty Wittmann, for making my recipes look so beautiful. I enjoyed every minute in the studio watching you two ladies work your magic. I am also eternally grateful to food photographers Lara Ferroni and Clare Barboza for generously donating their time, advice, and photography equipment(!) so I could contribute the chapter opening photos to *The Newlywed Kitchen*—something I would not have been able to do without your patient guidance.

To the couples who took the time to contribute their love stories to this project, and to Ali Basye for capturing their stories in such a lovely way—a warm thank-you!

I would also like to offer my sincere thanks to all my recipe testers, in particular an ex-pat living in Japan named Rona, who emailed me to tell me she somehow stretched the lemon pound cake recipe in this book so all sixty of her colleagues could have a taste, and how they raved about the recipe. Your emails were a constant source of encouragement! Thanks so much, all of you, who took the time to offer your comments and to photograph your efforts in the kitchen.

A special, heartfelt thanks to Shauna James Ahern, an incredible woman who has guided me through this process with the love and patience of a dear friend and mentor. To my dear family, particularly my mom and dad, who helped me cultivate a love for good food and cooking at an early age; I hope this cookbook does you proud!

And lastly (it seems fitting that I am writing my thank-yous on the eve of our first anniversary): to Henry, my incredible, loving husband, who has held my hand every step of the way; tasted, offered opinions, and dissected each and every one of my recipes; and put up with a messy kitchen for months on end. Here's to our first year of marriage, and to many happy years to come!

—Lorna

As with every project, the efforts of a number of generous people were essential in bringing this book to fruition, especially Tara Spicer, Gary Luke, Lorna Yee, Alexis Constantine, Rachelle Longé, Kathryn Barnard, Patty Wittmann, Diane Sepanski, Kate Basart, Michael Townley, Carilyn Platt, and Kim Ricketts. Special thanks goes to all of the couples who contributed their food/love stories—you are an inspiration—to Rachel Hart for mentoring me through the wedding world and beyond, and to Todd Davis, who happily cooks with love alongside me and for me.

—Ali

Index

Note: Photographs are indicated by *italics*.

About the Authors

Lorna Yee is a food writer for *Seattle* magazine. She cooked for two years at a popular, private underground dinner club. She is a newlywed and lives with her husband and her beloved puppy, Kimchee, in Seattle. Lorna blogs at www.thecookbookchronicles.com, a site that focuses on dining, food photography, home cooking, and farmers markets.

Ali Basye is a freelance writer and editor, the editor of *Seattle Bride* magazine, and the author of *The Long and Short of It: The Madcap History of the Skirt*.